Yoga
AND THE
Bible

Yoga
AND THE
Bible

THE YOGA OF THE DIVINE WORD

An explanation of vital Bible truths as taught by the perfect spiritual masters of the east. An introduction of the yoga or spiritual science of the true masters, who teach the path of spiritual attainment that is based upon the Word or Logos of the Bible.

Those who have been seeking a real master will here learn how to find him; and those who do not know if real masters exist on earth will here find evidence of interest to every sincere enquirer.

Joseph Leeming

RADHA SOAMI SATSANG BEAS

Published by:
Jagdish Chander Sethi, Secretary
Radha Soami Satsang Beas
Dera Baba Jaimal Singh
Punjab 143 204, India

Ninth edition 2004

11 10 09 08   8 7 6 5 4 3 2

ISBN 978-81-8256-043-7

Printed in India by: Lakshmi Offset Printers

*This book is humbly dedicated
with deep love and reverence to
Maharaj Charan Singh Ji
at whose suggestion
and with whose guidance and inspiration
it was written.*

CONTENTS

PREFACE TO THE SECOND EDITION

This book was first published in England in 1963 by the firm of George Allen & Unwin Ltd. This company specialises in publishing books on Yoga and metaphysical subjects, and through its branches situated throughout the world the present volume reached spiritual seekers in many countries. The response received from these readers shows that *Yoga and the Bible* serves a useful purpose in pointing out the fact that the spiritual teachings of Jesus and the founders of the other major world religions are the same as those that have been given out through the centuries by the many truly great Masters of India, Persia and other eastern countries.

Many western readers have reported that the book has been of particular value in "bridging the gap" between the teachings of the Christian religion and the teachings which today are imparted by the Masters of what has always been the highest form of Yoga taught in the East. This is Shabd Yoga, the Yoga of the Divine Word or Logos of the Bible, which is the creative and sustaining power and life-force of the Supreme Father.

It is because the present work has apparently been able to explain many basic religious and spiritual truths to those interested in discovering the real meaning of the highest system of Yoga, that it is now, with the consent of the author, being reprinted in India. It is hoped that it will continue to be of help to those who are looking for the highest form of Yoga, and that it will continue to aid readers in discovering the similarity of this age-old Yoga with the teachings of Jesus as given in the New Testament.

K.L. Khanna,
Secretary

Radha Soami Satsang Beas
1967

FOREWORD

I consider it my great good fortune to have been granted an opportunity to give my humble contribution to the Foreword of this book for which I am greatly beholden to my revered Master.

For many years it has been my privilege, together with many others both in India and abroad, to be a disciple of a perfect spiritual Master of the Radha Soami faith or spiritual science. During these years, I have watched men and women of all classes sit humbly in an attitude of sublimation and reverence at the feet of the Masters listening with rapt attention to their discourses concerning the subject matter of this book. This Radha Soami faith or spiritual science is above all castes, creeds, colour, race, and climes, leading men to immortality and eternal bliss.

In the east, the essence of these teachings is widely known and accepted as the veritable expression of spiritual truth, the true explanation of the purpose of our life on earth, and of our ultimate spiritual destiny. Some of the facts presented here may be new to western readers. But they are well comprehended by great numbers in the east. Rightly considered, they should expand the reader's knowledge towards a more comprehensive understanding of the order of the universe and the divine plan for mankind's spiritual salvation.

The contents of this book are based on discourses and writings of Masters of this spiritual path who are very well known in India. There is no expression of personal opinion on the part of the writer.

The living Master of the present day referred to in this book — Maharaj Charan Singh Ji of Beas, Punjab[1] — is venerated and

---

1. Maharaj Charan Singh Ji passed away on June 1, 1990. Two days before departing, He appointed Shri Gurinder Singh Ji as His successor.

honoured throughout India and in other eastern countries, as well as by those who are his followers in Europe, Africa and America. His genuine Mastership is acknowledged and attested to by tens of thousands in all parts of this country who have been accepted by him as disciples. He is revered and loved in India for his noble and benign human qualities, and inexpressibly more for his unquestioned spiritual powers. In him we see a sage who can awaken in man the spark of divine light and give the right conditions for the flame to blaze forth until all the lower propensities and desires are sublimated. He is serene and calm, illuminating the way for bewildered humanity to attain union with the divinity.

The Master represents the essential and unchanging truth of the ancient spiritual wisdom of India. In this age of doubt, scepticism, strife, hurry, religious controversy, ritual and ceremony, he comes with his message direct from the realms of the spirit, calling men and women away from the din and strife of tongues into the peaceful path of stillness within their own souls. 'The light that lighteth every man that cometh into the world' ever burns steadily and surely for all who will turn their weary eyes from the strife without to the quiet within. His teachings bear evidence of his communion with God and of his supreme ability to reveal spiritual truths. They possess a compelling power to answer the questions of the seeker, to put an end to doubts, and to bring peace of mind and soul. Thus, he is like a shade-giving tree in a thirsty land, or a sheltering rock in a storm.

The Master teaches that the soul of man is divine, and one in essence with the Supreme Creator. This divinity may be temporarily obscured, but can never be lost. It is the Master's function to teach man how to realise his own innate divinity, and to show him the way to God-realisation and to what is called in the western world 'Salvation' or 'Liberation'. This the Master does with unerring love and certitude, as can be testified to by many thousands in this country. Our revered Master is verily the ocean of life; beneath the turbulent waves, beyond the reach of tempests, he abides in the eternal calm.

Mr Joseph Leeming was initiated into the Radha Soami faith in the year 1954, and since then he has made six visits to the Radha

Soami Colony at Beas to study and assimilate the teachings at first
hand. During one of these visits we had the privilege of welcoming
him, together with our revered Master, at Sangli, where we had
many discussions on the various aspects of the spiritual science of
the Masters — the yoga of the divine Word.

Mr Leeming impressed me as a very sincere and thorough
student with a keen and trained intellect and an extensive knowledge
of eastern philosophies and religions. These qualities enabled him
to understand the teachings very accurately and comprehensively,
and to assess their value as compared to other systems of spiritual
knowledge known and taught in the east. I can say that he has
carefully analysed every aspect of this teaching. He has not accepted
it blindly, but has systematically considered and weighed every
point.

I am happy to write the foreword to this book, knowing that
every word contained in it is factual, accurate, and true to my
knowledge. It is hoped that it may aid in introducing the living
Master and the spiritual science which he and all other perfect
Masters have taught, to those in the English speaking world who
are searching for the light of spiritual wisdom, understanding, and
achievement.

C.A. Patwardhan
Raja of Sangli

Captain His Highness Raja Shrimant
Sir Chintamanrao
Appasaheb Patwardhan, KCSI, KCIE,
Raja of Sangli

1967

INTRODUCTION

This book is written primarily for the peoples of the west who, unlike many in the east, may be unfamiliar with its subject matter. Its purpose is to present in simple language some of the basic principles of the Yoga or spiritual science of the Masters, which has been taught for many centuries by the truly spiritual Masters of the east. Though little realised in the west, this Yoga is closely similar in essence to the basic spiritual teachings given in the Christian Bible.

In recent years 'Yoga' has become a familiar term in the western world. Most westerners, however, know of or practice the postures of Hatha Yoga, which is the lowest form of yogic spiritual discipline. Hatha yoga is very beneficial in promoting bodily health and mental serenity, but plays only a minor role in developing the higher spiritual consciousness.

Four other major forms of yoga are fairly widely known in the western world. These are :

1. Bhakti Yoga, the yoga of devotion. It discards all rites and ceremonies and seeks union with the Lord through the force of love only.

2. Karma Yoga, the yoga of action. It enjoins upon its followers the necessity of doing one's duty, whatever that may be; but without fear of blame or expectation of rewards. The essence of Karma yoga is the ideal of duty well done and the spirit of unattachment. It rejects the idea of renunciation and insists that one play one's part to the fullest extent without looking to the fruit of actions.

3. Jnana Yoga. This yoga seeks to concentrate and still the mind by easy and natural methods of mental discipline and control. The emphasis is upon the mind, rather than the body.

4. Ashtang or eightfold Yoga, also called Raja Yoga, the system described by the ancient Indian sage, Patanjali. This is a

comprehensive system of yoga training, which embraces both physical postures and mental disciplines. Many of its devotees rise to relatively high states of spiritual consciousness.

The yoga of the divine Word, or Shabd (divine sound) Yoga, described in these pages, is the highest of the Indian yoga systems. Its aim is entirely spiritual and its purpose is to enable the devotee to achieve salvation or liberation while living here on earth. Its system of meditation and other spiritual practices takes its followers to the highest attainable states of spiritual consciousness.

Nothing contained in this book is the mere opinion or idea of the writer. He makes no claim for himself and takes no credit whatever. Every fact presented and every statement made is taken from the teachings of the Masters, who speak not of what they believe, but of what they themselves experience and see and therefore know at first hand. And every fact and every statement has been demonstrated to be true over and over again, times without number, by the Masters and their disciples both in the past and in this present, practical twentieth century.

This book, in short, is not a compilation of theories or speculations. It is a statement of facts. If there are those who may not be able to believe them, these facts do not therefore lose one iota of their truth.

Some of the statements contained in the book may appear dogmatic, or even unbelievable, to those who meet them here for the first time. That is, in all probability, unavoidable. But in studying the teaching of the Masters, it is urged that for the time being at least the reader should try to divest himself of all prejudice and adopt an attitude of open-minded enquiry. He should not shut the door in his own face by assuming in advance that there is nothing new to be learned. For most of us there are yet 'many things in heaven and earth' not dreamed of in our philosophy.

Man in his search for truth has misinterpreted much and has often been unwilling to accept anything save that which comes to him surrounded by an aura of ancient tradition. For the most part, people on this small earth are materialistically minded. They have been so taught by precept and example. The concepts of the higher life that are available to them have been so vague that often the

teachings have been rejected when, at the same time, there has
been a deep desire for knowledge of how life should be lived to
fulfil man's destiny and the Creator's purpose.

If the reader discovers that the teaching described in this book
is of vital interest to him, he could do no better than adopt the
attitude of the great scientist Alexander Agassiz, who said :

'Let the scientific student sit down before the facts, as a little
child, and enquire of them.'

This is the necessary attitude, and it is welcomed by the Masters.
They ask anyone who is sincerely interested to come into the
laboratory of individual experiment and experience, and there
prove for themselves the truth of these teachings.

There is never any question of proselytising in connection with
the work of the Masters. Such an activity is of no use and is not
permitted in this field of enquiry. But those who are not satisfied
with abstractions and speculations, who have been searching for
specific and practical guidance in spiritual matters, and who feel
that there must be something more to be learned than is obtainable
from present-day religions or philosophies, may find what they
seek in the Spiritual Science described in this book.

In an effort to make the spiritual principles presented here more
readily understandable to those who are unacquainted with them,
the familiar sayings of Jesus are used throughout the book. These
are known to all western readers, and at the same time they
express the same fundamental truths that have been taught by all
truly spiritual Masters of all ages.

The meaning of these truths is then discussed as they have been
explained by past and present Masters of the east. It will be found
that their teachings and those of Jesus are essentially similar.

Many of the sayings of the eastern Masters are included as of
interest to the reader and because many western students have
found it helpful to see the truths given by Jesus stated in the terms
used by other great Masters. Included among these are a number
of statements quoted from the *Adi Granth,* which is the scripture
of the Sikh religion. Though little known in the west, it is one of
the world's most remarkable holy books, containing numerous
illuminating discussions of true spirituality and the methods by

which it is attained. The *Adi Granth* was compiled by the sixteenth-century Master, Guru Arjun Dev and some of his successors. Other quotations are taken from the *Bhagavad Gita,* which is as honoured among Hindus as a true guide to spiritual living and advancement as is the New Testament among Christians. The writer wishes to acknowledge his debt to other books written in English about the teaching of the Masters, without which the present work could not have been prepared. He is particularly indebted to Dr Julian P. Johnson, who, under the inspiration of Huzur Maharaj Sawan Singh Ji, One of the greatest of recent Masters, wrote *With a Great Master in India,* and *The Path of the Masters.* Other works that have been of special value include *Spiritual Gems,* a collection of letters by the Master Sawan Singh; *Light on Sant Mat* by the Master Charan Singh; the *Sar Bachan,* or 'Essence of the Teachings', by the nineteenth-century Master, Huzur Soami Ji Maharaj of Agra, who in this book is called simply Soami Ji the title by which he is known today in India; and *Mysticism, the Spiritual Path,* by Lekh Raj Puri.

JOSEPH LEEMING

1963

CHAPTER 1

SEEK AND YE SHALL FIND

'Ask and it shall be given you; seek, and ye shall find; knock, and it shall be opened unto you. For every one that asketh receiveth; and he that seeketh findeth; and to him that knocketh, it shall be opened.'

—*Matthew 7 : 7-8*

These words speak of the deep longing of the soul for a higher and more perfect life so keenly felt by thoughtful persons everywhere today, and known to spiritual aspirants in all ages of the world's long history.

They speak of the age-old spiritual quest of man, his never ending search for the truths of human and eternal life, and for the abiding reality above and beyond the triviality of human existence.

Men and women throughout the world today are searching, perhaps more earnestly than ever before, for the basic truths of life and the ultimate meaning of human existence. Many are longing for certainty in a world where it often seems that the only certain thing is uncertainty. 'For change alone is constant,' as the poet says. In the western countries of today particularly, life seems to contain everything—except meaning. In spite of his intellectual and scientific advancement, the modern man is still groping in the dark insofar as spiritual matters are concerned, and does not know where to seek the light.

Modern man has found that material progress, however useful it may be, does nothing to satisfy his deeper aspirations.

And largely as a result of scientific progress, man today is troubled and unhappy, and lives in fear rather than in hope as he looks towards the future. Man's knowledge of the visible material world has increased to an almost unimaginable extent; but his knowldege of the invisible worlds of the spirit is less, perhaps, than in any previous period of history.

Right-minded persons in all countries today are troubled by the crumbling of traditional values, the spiritual disorientation and the moral degradation seen in the present-day world, and are striving to find dependable spiritual values for themselves. For even in this twentieth-century materialistic and scientific world, men and women still feel that they have souls. But this feeling by itself is of little practical help. Those who are touched with spiritual longing still ponder the question : what shall we do to find our souls?

And positive and practical answers are needed for the other basic questions raised—but not always solved to everyone's satisfaction—by religion and philosophy. Why are we here, and what is the object and purpose of our existence? What is the ultimate goal of human yearning and effort? What shall we do to be 'saved'? Is there anyone anywhere who knows what we should do in order to realise, with certainty and without fail, the promises held out by religion—salvation, entrance into the kingdom of heaven, and reunion with the Supreme Father?

No questions of greater importance confront a human being than those of discovering who and what he really is, what place he occupies in the universe, what his relationship is to the Supreme Creator, and what path he should follow to 'do the Father's will' and gain what in the Bible is called salvation.

Masters of Today

Is there in the world today any source of positive

knowledge concerning these fundamental questions of human and spiritual life?

The answer is, yes. The words of Jesus are as true today, and true in exactly the same manner, as they were when he spoke them. The kingdom of heaven is at hand, today as yesterday, and there are those now living here on earth who can show the seeker how to enter it. There is today, as there always has been, a practical method whereby the spiritually hungry can be fed.

For there are on earth today, as there have been in all past ages, perfect Masters who *know* the answers to these questions and to all the other basic questions for which mankind seeks the answers.

This is not only true, but is also eminently logical, provided one's mind is not closed by lifelong prejudices. If we acknowledge the fact that God sent one beloved Son to aid struggling mankind, is it not entirely reasonable to accept the fact that God can still show us His infinite love in the same manner?

Actually there is no statement in the New Testament, except possibly one or two interpolations, in which Jesus makes any claim to an exclusive divine sonship. This idea was not incorporated into the Christian religion until long after his death.

'It is a fatal error to assume that there is, and can be, only one Christ, or divine son,' says Dr Julian P. Johnson in his book, *With a Great Master in India.* 'By such an assumption a man shuts the door of opportunity in his own face. Besides, for such an assumption, there is no rational need. It is utterly without reason or fact to support it. It accomplishes no good purpose, while doing vast harm'.

'It is, moreover, a poor and limited view of the Supreme Father. Indeed, poor in resources would He be, if He were so limited that He could send into this world only one great

Teacher during all the millions of years of its history.'

Guru Nanak, a great Indian Master, says: 'At all times He keeps Saints in the world, to carry on His mission of Grace.'

The Supreme Father's love and power are boundless, and the purpose of His divine plan is to bring back to their original home those who have become ready to return as a result of their experiences on earth. This return can be achieved only with the help and guidance of a living Master. Accordingly, as part of the divine plan, there have always been on earth one or more living Masters, to whom mankind— the prodigal sons of God—could turn for help.

Many in the east and an increasing number in the west are now aware of this fact. Many westerners, however, brought up in the Christian faith, hesitate to approach a living Master, believing that by doing so they will have to give up their own religion. Nothing could be farther from the truth.

It has been the common experience of western disciples of the living Masters of today to find that their veneration for the beloved Master Jesus has become immeasurably greater as they have come to have a deeper and more comprehensive understanding of the true nature of his divinity and his mission. From the teachings of their own Masters and from the spiritual progress they have made as a result of these teachings, they now understand and know more of the love, compassion, mercy, and radiant spirituality of Jesus, and of the other great Masters who have been sent to earth by the one great Father of us all.

No one, therefore, has to give up his devotion to Jesus if he walks on the path of the living Masters. By this path, in fact, he becomes a better Christian. In the same way, the Masters point out, a Hindu becomes a better Hindu, a Muslim a better Muslim, and a Buddhist a better Buddhist.

Moreover, a follower of any religion may study with the Masters without alienating himself from his own religion or without ceasing to attend his own church services. The Masters do not establish new creeds or churches, and are friendly towards all existing religions. They are concerned only with helping their followers to achieve genuine spiritual advancement. It is a private, individual matter and has to do only with the student's search for spiritual truth.

The disciples of a living Master, as was the case with the disciples of Jesus, do not have to rely on guesswork, speculation, fine-spun theories, or blind belief. No longer are they obliged to take the promises of religion on faith alone, with no positive or conclusive assurance of their truth. They know and have incontrovertible proof, through their own inner spiritual experiences, that these promises are true and can be realised here and now. A fairer and a finer life has begun for them, and they have started on their journey home, the ultimate destiny of all mankind.

These statements may sound surprising to those who are not acquainted with the Masters and their work. But they are based on the experience of many thousands—even hundreds of thousands—of persons who are living in the world today. Most of these are in India and other eastern countries where knowledge of the spiritual path that leads to the kingdom of heaven has been kept alive throughout all the centuries of the world's known history. But today, also, there is a large and constantly expanding group of disciples in the western lands, who are proving by their own direct experience that the promises of Jesus and other great spiritual Masters are facts which can be tested, proved, and realised, not in the hereafter, but here and now.

The testing and proving of the statements made by the Masters can be accomplished, moreover, by anyone who elects to follow the prescribed path. Whoever, after due deliberation and of his own free will and choice, takes to this path and follows it with full sincerity and devotion will be able to prove for himself that the kingdom of heaven is at hand, that immortal life is a reality, that true salvation can be achieved, and that life can be filled with a happiness, joy, and certainty far greater than any ever known before. As one progresses on the path, he too will in time be able to say, not 'I believe', but 'I know'.

The Seekers

For most people, the first step is the search of which Jesus spoke, a seeking for something in which one can believe without doubt; something that does not have to be accepted on blind faith alone; something that will not only uplift and spiritualise the heart, the mind, and the soul, but which, while transcending reason and intelligence, will also satisfy them.

There are many who can no longer find satisfaction in the tenets of the organised religions. Evidence of this fact can be found in the very great numbers of people—many thousands in all of the major nations of the world—who have been moved to search for spiritual knowledge and a way of salvation that they cannot find by conforming to the doctrines and rituals of organised religious bodies.

In the world at large, the seekers are not numerous. They are the rare souls who, as a rule, have come to this life with spiritual tendencies. Krishna says in the *Bhagavad Gita* (The Song Celestial):

'Among thousands of men, one perchance strives for perfection'.

Relatively few are really earnest in their search for the truly spiritual path. Absorbed in the seeming reality of the material world, the vast majority are quite content to bury themselves in its spiritually deadening satisfactions. But beyond the day-to-day routine of ordinary existence, there is a higher and far finer way of life. And when man finally understands the truth of his spiritual origin, he begins to understand the underlying and all-important purpose of his human life on earth. This purpose is spiritual growth.

Throughout the ages the seekers, sensing the existence of this higher life, have cried out to God as did the writer of one of India's *Upanishads* thousands of years ago :

> 'From the unreal lead us to the Real,
> From darkness lead us to the Light,
> From death lead us to Immortality.'

The seekers have realised that the material world is not the only world. They realise that the unaided intellect of man alone can never provide the answers to their questions. They sense that what we see is only a fraction of what really is. Glimpsing the truth, haunted by the pettiness and emptiness of life, they are driven to search for the spiritual reality and purpose behind the seeming lack of meaning in ordinary human existence.

The spiritual science of the Masters enables the sincere seeker to see deeper into life, to understand the spiritual purpose behind mundane affairs, and to comprehend the divine harmony and meaning underlying all the surface discords of human life. It confirms through personal experience the claims that are the essence of Christianity and all other world religions. And it satisfies to the full the deepest longings and loftiest aspirations of man's being.

A deep and abiding longing for spiritual truth and spiritual experience are indications that one is a true seeker and is on the path towards initiation by a perfect Master.

But whether or not one is now ready cannot be known until one meets the Master, for this can be determined only by the Master himself. In actual practice today, however, among people of good character and of high intelligence, it seldom happens that anyone who asks for initiation is not fit for the path. If he is not ready, he will not knock at the door.

Those who do knock are, as a rule, those who have spent much of their lives in a search for the truth and who have found life in this world to be a hard and bitter experience. It is trite but true, that man's extremity is God's opportunity.

When the seeker is in right earnest, it is a strong indication that he is ready for the path. 'If you are in right earnest to be good and pure, God will send you that Sat Guru (True Light-Giver), the right teacher. Earnestness is the one thing necessary,' says Sri Ramakrishna, the nineteenth-century sage of Bengal.

For such a one, even the smallest hint that there are living Masters is usually enough. But if one has only intellectual interest or curiosity about the subject, no amount of argument or discussion will avail to make him seek out a Master. It is still true, as in the days of the Hebrew prophet Jeremiah, that:

> 'Ye shall seek me, and find me, (only) when ye shall search for me with all your heart.'
>
> *Jeremiah 29 : 13*

Many have found that the search is a long one. Years are spent in studying the literature of different religions, both of the west and of the east, of different systems of Yoga and occultism; and of the various groups and societies that endeavour to explain the mysteries and meaning of human existence and of man's relationship to God. Whole libraries of books may be read in the effort to find a clue, and all that is gained are theories or opinions. Time and again the seeker may cry out with the great metaphysical poet John Donne:

> 'Oh, what a dusty answer gets the Soul,
> When hot for certainty in this our life.'

Often the search may seem hopeless and the seeker may be tempted to abandon it, only at last to learn with unexpected suddenness that there are living Masters and there is a Way.

In the end, those who genuinely long for the great treasure of spiritual truth, the pearl of great price, and search for it with unflagging perseverance will find it, as Jesus promised that they would. But the longing must be genuine. That is the only way, and it is the right way. For knowledge to a certain extent is hidden, in order to ward off the superficially curious enquirers and those who are not yet ready.

The promise of Jesus that those who seek will find may be compared with the well-known eastern precept:

> 'When the chela (disciple) is ready, the Guru (Master or literally Light-Giver) appears.'

Those who long to become *chelas,* or disciples of a true spiritual Master, are the seekers. If they succeed in finding a genuine Master their search will be at an end, for the Master will show them the way to the eternal light of God. The Master, moreover, will be a living Master, one who walks the earth today, followed and loved and worshipped by his disciples, as was Jesus some two thousand years ago. For a living Master is needed to set the disciple's feet on the path.

In the past the search for a genuine Master was purposely made more difficult than it is today. Disciples were accepted only after the most severe tests. Now the Masters have modified this policy. During recent years they have accepted practically all who have applied for initiation, unless their karmas—their deeds in earlier lives—have been too evil. This is partly because there are many more seekers today who have reached the point of being ready for the path.

Actually, the Masters themselves continually watch over those who are aspiring for a higher life and seeking as best they can to find the way. Just as a man standing on the summit of a hill in the darkness of the night can see lights that are shining in many near and far-distant places, so can the Masters see the light within a true seeker after God. When that light is bright and strong enough and the aspirant is ready, the Master sees to it that he is brought into contact with himself.

This truth is beautifully expressed in the parable of the prodigal son, in which Jesus said:

> 'But when he was yet a great way off, his father saw him and had compassion.
>
> *Luke 15 : 20*

The contact may be made through a friend, through a chance acquaintance, or by some other means. 'God moves in a mysterious way, His wonders to perform.' But wherever the aspirant may be, even on the remotest isle of the sea, the Master will seek him out and make a way to tell him of the path.

Fortunate above all others is the seeker who finds a true Master and is accepted by him into his fold. This is the greatest boon that can come to any man or woman. For when one finds a perfect Master, he finds true happiness and the truth of truths which struggling and despairing mankind has sought throughout the ages. The final liberation of his soul from the dark worlds of matter is then absolutely assured. Nothing in the universe can possibly defeat that end. Out of his boundless love and compassion for suffering humanity, the Master will place the disciple's feet on the path that leads to eternal life.

So we may lift up our hearts and know that, with the help of a living Master, we will be shown the path and our spiritual progress will be assured. With the help of a living Master, the Way is opened to the eternal life which is enduring treasure.

CHAPTER 2

MY DOCTRINE IS HIS THAT SENT ME

'Jesus answered them, and said, My doctrine is not mine, but his that sent me. If any man will do his will, he shall know of the doctrine, whether it be of God, or whether I speak of myself.'

—*John 7 : 16-17*

The great Masters of all ages have all taught the same doctrine, the identical method of freeing the soul from the fetters of mind and matter and of entering the kingdom of heaven while still living on earth in the physical body. The Way that was taught by Jesus to his closest disciples is the Way that is taught today by the perfect living Masters.

The Way is called here the path of the Masters or, because it is a scientific method of achieving continuous and certain spiritual progress and successively higher states of consciousness, it is called the spiritual science of the Masters. In India it is sometimes called Sant Mat, which means the Way or Teachings of the Saints. Sant means a Master of the highest order. Mat means philosophy, knowledge. Sant Mat refers to the philosophy or teachings of the Masters based on knowledge gained by direct personal experience. In the present times it is comprehensively propounded by the Radha Soami teachings, Radha Soami being an appellation of the Supreme and nameless creator, God. Its literal meaning is lord of the soul, Radha meaning soul, and Soami meaning lord.

The spiritual science or yoga of the Masters, the doctrine of Him who sends the Masters to this world, is the supreme science of all sciences, for it deals with the ultimate truths of man's nature and destiny, and the ultimate purpose of all human life. It teaches the student, by a method of guided scientific experimentation, how to make *direct* and permanent contact with his Creator. It is a science based on laws which, though they have always existed, are not generally known. And it is the greatest of all sciences, because it turns ordinary mortals into divine beings.

'Briefly', says one of the greatest Masters of recent times, Huzur Baba Maharaj Sawan Singh Ji, 'it is a practical method of separating the soul from its combination with the mind and the body, and then uniting it with its Source, or the Supreme Creator.'

It has also been described as 'a scientific and spiritual method of entering and realising the kingdom of heaven while still living here in the human body.'

If a method of spiritual growth and the development of a higher life and consciousness are to be considered not as mere words, but as a practical and scientific system, it must provide indisputable evidence to prove its validity to all who are willing to try and test it. This, the science of the Masters does. For the attainment of higher states of consciousness, liberation from the bondage of mind and matter, and entry into the kingdom of heaven while still living here on earth are not empty theories or matters of wishful thinking. They are specific accomplishments that can be achieved, tested, and proved by all who are willing to follow the simple rules laid down by the true Masters.

No blind belief or blind faith is called for when one is following this path. As the student follows the instructions given by the Master at the time of initiation and subsequently, he obtains through his own inner experiences definite proof of his spiritual progress and positive confirmation of the truths enunciated by Jesus and all other great spiritual teachers.

Some of the facts comprised in the teaching will be new to many, but they call for no credulity. While the teaching sets forth some basic truths that are not generally known in the west, it asks no acceptance on faith alone. Instead, it offers a method by which the interested student may prove for himself each and every assertion that it makes. It proposes nothing that is to be believed without ample evidence. It is a scientific method that yields verifiable results with precision.

We live today in a predominantly scientific and intellectual age and our times demand a sensible and rational explanation of spiritual matters. Many have found this rational and scientific explanation in the spiritual science of the Masters.

Whoever studies and practises this science with the help and guidance of a properly qualified teacher, will receive increasing confirmation of the existence of God and the truth of his own divinity through his own first-hand experience. The science of the Masters is thus an empirical science, based on verification through personal experience. Its methods are exact and its results uniform. In all ages of the world, among all races and in all countries, all who follow its methods achieve exactly the same results.

The fact that the spiritual work of the Masters is an exact science is quite difficult for some in the west to grasp, accustomed as they are to thinking of religion and spirituality as matters of faith and belief alone. But the readers for whom this book is intended will find that the Masters' science contains the inner essence and truth of every extant world religion. And it gives its followers not only hope for the future, but positive certainty and present realisation.

This is possible because the Masters are not mere preachers, but may accurately be described as super-scientists. They have knowledge of laws of which the material scientists are totally unaware, and they use these laws to hasten the spiritual development of their disciples.

It has been said that a small amount of science—or philosophy—often leads to atheism; but a larger amount brings men back to God. The spiritual science of the Masters is the larger amount for which many have been seeking. For its purpose and the inevitable result of its practice is to lead men back to God.

While the teaching of the Masters goes far beyond that of any present-day world religion, there is little, if any, contradiction between it and the fundamental precepts of the organised religions. The sincere reader should bear this in mind and not permit preconceived dogmas to block his investigation. The path of the Masters is offered as a supplement to what he already possesses, no matter to what religious organisation he may belong. It does not wish or try to do away with what he already has, but aims to give him additional light by way of confirmation.

This is a study that offers the most valuable rewards to true scientific research, for it provides the means of securing man's deepest and most enduring happiness. It offers both consolation and certitude, both peace of mind and peace of soul, to those who are in distress, for it proves that there is a way open to all—and open now—leading to the everlasting life which is enduring treasure and eternal joy.

The material science of today undertakes to trace everything to physical causes, which are perceptible to the human senses and mind. But the science of the Masters teaches and demonstrates that the principal and basic cause of everything is the imperceptible and all-powerful Spirit. And by its method of scientific demonstration it provides the most positive proofs of everything that is claimed by any religion, and then goes far beyond them all.

As Jesus said, this path is not the doctrine of any individual Master, but the doctrine of the Supreme Father, who sends the Masters to the world in order to help mankind. It is the method of approach and return to God established, not by man, but by the Supreme Creator Himself.

It is as old as creation, having been taught by the Masters since the beginning of human life. For human beings of superior intelligence have lived on this earth for an infinitely longer period of time than present day scientists and archaeologists imagine. This path, in more recent times, was the secret of the highest mysteries of ancient Egypt and Greece.

It is a perfect method, which has not changed in the past and will not change in the future, because it has been a perfect science since the beginning, instituted and practised by perfect men of God who never make mistakes. The study of the writings of the Sages shows that no matter in what age or country they appeared, they all followed and revealed to the world this same spiritual Way. The Way has always been the same because it is God's plan for the redemption of all mankind.

For these reasons the spiritual yoga of the Masters has, by some, been called 'God's own religion'.

How this is so will become clear as one reads and understands the facts given in these pages. In speaking of these truths, the Master Sawan Singh says:

> This method of spiritual uplift is natural, within all, designed by God, and as old as creation itself. It is the design of the Creator, and none can alter, amend or add to it. It is as ancient as man. The Creator, when He created man, designed this Path in him.

Ages ago, long, long before the founders of the earliest religions such as the Buddha, Zoroaster and the unknown writers of the Vedas, this simple truth was known and taught that man, when aided by a perfect Master, can consciously unite with the divine while living in the physical body.

The teaching of the Masters is sometimes called a religion, but, unlike the orthodox religions, it has no organisation, no priests, no dogmas, no ritual, no ceremony, and requires nothing to be believed without evidence. Its entire structure is based upon positive knowledge, which any student may demonstrate for himself. Thus, it differs significantly from those religions whose followers are accustomed to placing their reliance on belief and faith alone. The system is strictly a scientific one and, at the same time, it is the very essence of real religion.

Every religion has two aspects—the outer or exoteric, and the inner or esoteric. The history of religions shows us that in the beginning each one centred about a spiritualised God-man or Master, one who was in close and constant unity with God. To him was given the mission of preaching the doctrine, and the power of bringing his followers into touch with the inner reality, of teaching them how they could rise up, enter the kingdom of heaven, and commune with their Creator.

This esoteric form of the teachings continued as long as the Master or his spiritually advanced successors were on earth to teach and guide spiritual seekers. But when the leadership passed into the hands of those who were less spiritually advanced, and lost the spiritual presence and power of the God-man who was the original preceptor, the path lost the power of giving its followers direct and conscious contact with their Creator. Thereafter, by degrees it became largely a matter of creeds, dogmas, prayers, rites and ceremonies. Entering the kingdom of heaven then became largely a hope that might be realised after death, rather than a definite and vital personal experience here and now, made possible by the spiritual power of the living Master.

But there always are living Masters in the world, revealing the true spiritual way. There are such Masters even today, pointing out, with their divine power, the inner or esoteric path to those interested.

Many people in the western world who have heard or read of the path of the Masters have asked the pertinent question: what is its relation to Christianity?

The answer is this : "the path is identical with Christianity, if by that term we mean the spiritual teachings of Jesus. The teaching of the Masters does not change with time. It is the same in the past, the present, and the future. The living perfect Masters of today teach precisely the same spiritual truths as those that Jesus taught when he walked the earth."

The spiritual science of the Masters, however, is not Christianity, if by that term we mean the system of dogma and theology that was created by men other than Jesus during the centuries that followed his presence here on earth.

The esoteric or inner part of every existing world religion is one and the same. The spiritual truths, principles, and practices that underlie them are identical. These truths were taught by the founders of all the world religions, and are taught today by the living Masters who are now with us.

The Masters of Christianity, Judaism, Buddhism, Hinduism, Islam and Taoism taught in some degree the spiritual science of the Masters that is described in this book. A comparison of the statements contained in this book with those made by the Masters of the different world religions, who taught the esoteric truths, will show that this is the case.

In every instance, the esoteric teaching is not a man-made one, but a God-made one. For in each instance the founders of religions and the genuine Masters have taught, not their own doctrine, but the doctrine or system of Him who sent them to this world. And this is the age-old natural and perfect system designed by the Creator for the express purpose of liberating man from the bondage of the body and mind and enabling him to enter and enjoy the kingdom of heaven here and now as well as in the future. It is only the living Masters who can show us how to do this here and now, however, while all religions point to the hope of it after death.

CHAPTER 3

MANY MANSIONS

'In my Father's house are many mansions.'
—John 14 : 2
'Eye hath not seen, nor ear heard, neither have
entered into the heart of man, the things which
God hath prepared for them that love Him.'
—I Corinthians 2 : 9

To understand the work of the Masters and the ultimate purpose and goal of human life, it is necessary to have at least an outline knowledge of the structure of the great universe of universes, of which the physical universe is but the lowest, darkest, and smallest part. This information, as taught by the great Saints and Masters of the east, is given briefly here.

The extent of the total universe is far greater and more vast than is imagined by present-day scientists or by the majority of the men and women who now live in this world. For above and beyond the material universe of stars, suns, planets and galaxies known to the astronomers, there exists an almost endless number of higher and finer worlds that no astronomer can see, no matter how powerful his telescope. Guru Nanak says :

'There are millions of skies and millions of universes,
Whose numbers the pandits and the wise fail to count.'

And Maulana Rum declares :

'The intellect and brain become paralysed when trying to comprehend the extent of His creation.
This universe would seem like a hair in an ocean.'

These higher worlds are beyond the reach of any man-made instrument, for they are beyond the borders of the material universe and are composed of finer substance that is not discoverable by material means. But the Masters are thoroughly familiar with them, for they visit them again and again, day after day. They have passed through them times without number, and they know them as well as we know the different parts of this world in which we have lived or which we have visited many times. And many disciples of the Masters now living on this earth also make frequent, if not daily visits to these unimaginably beautiful higher worlds, each containing more light and beauty than the one below it, and providing a more happy existence for its inhabitants.

The Masters teach that the great universe is divided into four grand divisions. These are known as Sat Desh, meaning the real or abiding country; Brahmand, the region of Brahm or the Universal Mind; and, the astral region; and Pind, the physical universe. In each of these divisions there are several major regions, each of which is subdivided into almost numberless different subdivisions according to the degree of spirituality or transcendence they possess. These are the many mansions of the Father's house.

Sat Desh, the First Grand Division

In the highest heavenly region there is only pure spirit, unmixed with any sort of matter. It is the region of universal Spirit and there, in the purest and completely spiritual state of creation, the soul of man is at home and in its native element, ever sustained by the waves of life, love, and power that emanate from the Supreme Creator. This region is our true home, the name by which it is so often referred to by the Masters.

The Indian name for this highest grand division of the

great universe is Sat Desh, which means the real or abiding country. From here, the light, life, love, and power of the Supreme One flows outward and downward to permeate and sustain all the worlds below. The love and energy of this region permeate and interpenetrate everything in the regions below it.

Sat Desh is the region of truth, of ultimate reality, the supreme heaven of heavens. It is the dwelling place of an infinite number of pure spiritual beings or souls, possessed of God-like beauty and majesty, who know neither death, sorrow nor imperfection. Among them are many who have finished their earth lives and have returned to their spiritual home with the aid of a perfect Master. For all the Saints and perfect Masters either come from Sat Desh or through the power bestowed on them, have instant access to it, even while here on earth.

According to the Masters, these regions cannot be described with any degree of accuracy, since there are no thought-forms or words in human language that can express their wonders and their beauty. We who live in this low material world are too limited in comprehension. The great nineteenth century Saint, Soami Ji of Agra, when speaking of Sat Desh, said simply :

'What beauty and glory! How can I describe them? There is nothing here to convey the idea. Love plays the supreme part. It is all Love.'

This grand division is immeasurably vast, so illimitable in extent that no sort of understanding of its size can be conveyed to the human intelligence. All that the Masters can say of it is that it is limitless. At the same time, its light is so brilliant that a sun such as ours, but a thousand times larger, would appear as no more than a tiny dark spot.

An attempt to indicate its extent can be made by comparing

it with the physical universe, part of which can be seen by the world's astronomers. This contains countless billions of stars and galaxies, each galaxy being millions of light-years distant from any other. Some astronomers believe that there may be as many stars in the universe as there are grains of sand on the beaches of the world. Our sun, the centre of our solar system, is merely one of these stars. Yet if this entire vast physical universe were placed in Sat Desh, it would appear to be no more than a 'hair in an ocean'.

The higher worlds are often spoken of as planes, but the idea of horizontal planes one above the other does not give a true picture. Think rather of the physical universe, the lowest grand division, as a sphere, and then think of the higher worlds as increasingly larger spheres surrounding it on all sides and interpenetrating it.

An idea of the relative size of these spheres can be gained from the statement made by the Masters that the physical universe is but a drop in the ocean of Brahmand. This grand division, in turn, is but a drop in the limitless ocean of Sat Desh.

The highest region in Sat Desh is named by the Masters, Radha Soami Dham, meaning the abode of the Supreme Lord God, Radha Soami. It's also called 'Anami Lok'. It is the dwelling place of the Supreme Father who, though nameless (Anami), is also called Radha Soami or Lord of the Soul by the Saints and Masters. He is the beneficent creator and preserver of all that lives throughout the entire vast system of universes.

Brahmand, The Second Grand Division

The second grand division of the great universe is called by the Masters, Brahmand. The name means 'the egg of Brahm', and refers to its approximate shape which is roughly that of an elongated sphere.

The substance of Brahmand is mostly spirit, but with it there is mixed a certain amount of refined or spiritualised matter. It is the finest order of matter, and includes the matter that constitutes mind, which is extremely fine and mixed with spirit substance to some slight extent. It is called the 'spiritual-material' region, because spirit dominates. As one descends through it, however, drawing closer to the material worlds, its substance becomes coarser and more and more mixed with matter. In the lower portion of Brahmand mind is supreme over spirit.

This great region is vast in extent, beyond the power of the human mind to imagine, but it is very small in comparison with Sat Desh. Brahm is the ruler of the Three Worlds namely, Brahmand, And and Pind which, unlike Sat Desh, are subject to change and dissolution.

And, the Third Grand Division

This is the astral world, extending from the eye centre to the lower boundaries of Brahmand. On crossing the eye centre the soul steps into this region. The Astral Plane is resplendent and colorful, superior to anything ever seen on this earth. However, in comparison to Brahmand its brightness and beauty fade into insignificance.

Much more vast in extent than the physical universe, And has many subplanes, heavens and purgatories, numberless continents, rivers, mountains, oceans and cities— all abounding in an endless variety of life.

Its capital, called 'Sahasradal Kanwal', meaning 'a thousand-petalled lotus', constitutes the great cluster of lights, which is the 'powerhouse' of the entire physical universe. Out of this 'powerhouse' flows the power that sustains all the worlds, stars and planets in the physical region called Pind.

Like Brahmand, this region also is not immortal or imperishable —neither are its inhabitants.

Lying nearest to the physical region, And forms the port of entry for all higher regions. All souls who are journeying to higher regions must pass through it.

The happiness and bliss of this region is something the inhabitants of the physical universe can hardly imagine. Yet this is only the first station on the upward Path of the Masters.

The Physical Universe, the Fourth Grand Division

The fourth grand division is called by the Masters, Pind. It is the gross material or physical universe in which we now live. Here coarse matter predominates, with only a small amount of mind and a still smaller amount of spirit. The amount of spirit is just sufficient to maintain the life of the region, for it should be understood that spirit is the only real life that exists and all other life depends for its continued existence upon the animating power of spirit. Without spirit, matter is inert or dead. It is as Jesus said :

> 'It is the spirit that quickeneth; the flesh (matter) profiteth nothing.'
>
> *John 6 : 63*

This region contains all the stars and the suns and their planets, of which the earth is one. But all of the untold millions of suns, stars and galaxies now known to astronomers constitute only a very small portion of the grand total of the Pind region. There are millions more beyond the reach of the astronomers' telescopes.

The immensity of the physical universe staggers the human imagination. It is a universe in which our earth is a dwarf planet revolving about a dwarf star, a universe of myriads of planets, stars, and galaxies of unimaginably enormous size, separated from us and from each other by inconceivable distances, hurtling at tremendous speeds through immeasurable space.

Yet the entire area of Pind, the physical universe, is but little more than a few tiny specks of dust floating in the sky of Brahmand.

Pind is so deficient in spirit substance that it is in a state of semi-death, a condition of deep darkness and heavy inertia, as compared with the heavenly realms about it. It is this condition that gives rise to all the manifold difficulties experienced by mortals in these lower worlds, for the amount of true happiness, peace, harmony, and joy is determined by the amount of spirit that is present.

This world at best is only a feeble reflection of the sublime beauty and reality of the astral region and the finer worlds that lie above it. Of the real spiritual light there is no more than a feeble glimmering here and there in the almost universal darkness. It is probably the astral region that Plato called the 'World of Forms' compared to which he considered the physical world as a world of shadows.

From this brief description of the structure and extent of the great universe of universes, the reader may understand in some measure the incredible vastness of the many mansions of the Father's house and the small and humble position occupied in it by the physical universe and those who inhabit it.

CHAPTER 4

ALL THINGS WERE MADE BY HIM

*'In the beginning was the Word, and the Word was
with God, and the Word was God...All things were
made by him, and without him was not anything made
that was made. In him was life; and the life was the
light of men.'*

—John I : 1-4

These moving and meaningful statements made by St. John
in describing the Divine Word of God are among the best
known in the entire New Testament. But it is safe to say that
their true meaning is one of the least known of all facts in the
entire teachings of the Bible.

Should you ask any representative group of western
Christians the question: what did St. John mean by the Word
that was with God and was God? You would receive in all
probability a diversity of answers. A search through
encyclopaedias and books about the Christian religion would
yield a similar result. Of all the answers given, however, the
most frequent would probably be that the Word of God is the
Bible itself, which has often been called the revealed Word
of God. This meaning is probably the one most widely
accepted in the western world today.

To the spiritual Masters, of both the past and the present,
however, the Word referred to in this passage has a radically
different meaning. For they have always taught, as did Jesus
also, that the Word of God is not a spoken or written word
or teaching. It is something entirely different.

What, then is the Divine Word?

It is a power, the omnipresent and omnipotent creative and sustaining spiritual power of the Supreme Lord God. Emanating from the Creator in the form of a current or wave of spiritual vibrations of immeasurably powerful intensity, it flows outwards without ceasing to permeate and penetrate all worlds and all created things and beings.

This power is also referred to in the Bible as the Holy Spirit, the Holy Ghost, the Comforter and in some passages the Name of God.

St. John, in the opening sentences of his Gospel, speaks of the Word as the great creative current, the dynamic outpouring of the Supreme Father's power, as the Creator of all the grand divisions of the great universe, together with their numberless sub-divisions, their mighty rulers, and the countless multitudes of souls that inhabit them. It is the Word, the projected power of God, that created the universe, as St. John says; and it is this same power that now sustains it and the life of all things in it.

All life and energy in the universe come from the Divine Word. It is a power that is mightier than any known on earth, for it is the power behind all other powers. All other powers are finite, but this power is infinite. It is the one basic power in the universe. It shows itself in many apparently different forms of energy; but trace them back to their original source and they are all found to be fundamentally one—the dynamic power of God. It dwells hidden, but supremely active, at the back of all other energy.

The Word is the incalculable power that controls the movements of the suns and planets in their orbits. It is the tremendous power that binds together the particles in the nucleus of the atom—the greatest force as yet discovered by scientists of today. In it abides all the energy of the universe, either latent or dynamic. It requires only the proper conditions to express itself as dynamic force or, as some of the eastern Masters have called it, God in action. It has many forms of expression, most of which are as yet unknown to the scientists of today.

At this point it should be noted that this great power, the Divine Word of God, is the basic factor in the Yoga or spiritual science of the Masters. It is the very foundation of all true Masters' teachings, and the principal factor that distinguishes their method of spiritual development from all others. It is the one fact by which a real Master may be known, for no one is or can be a genuine Master unless he teaches and practises the Divine Word.

How the Masters use the Word in their great works here on earth is described throughout this book. That is indeed, a major purpose for which this book was written.

Like electricity in the air, the Word or Holy Spirit of God is everywhere present. It permeates the universe and is immanent in every individual and in every other created thing. Its omnipresence helps to explain the omnipresence of God.

In recent years the scientists have found that energy exists everywhere, and is present in every atom of matter throughout the universe. Einstein showed that matter and energy are actually only different forms of the same thing. Scientists no longer talk about matter and energy separately. They are identical, and this is so because all matter is built up of atoms that contain the boundless energy of God. Everything that exists in the material world is energy, electric vibration in one or another form. Even the very stones and rocks are interpenetrated by the God-life of their atoms. So tremendous is this power that according to the scientists, enough of it is locked up in a teaspoonful of water to raise a load of five million tons from sea level to the top of Mount Everest.

The atomic discoveries of the scientists point to God in

action, in all matter, though they do not as yet realise this fact. It is of great interest, however, that the results of their research into the laws and nature of the physical universe question the reality of matter and show energy to be the basis of the universe. Some among the scientists have stated their belief that this tremendous energy is the mysterious power of God. But they are in a minority. The Masters speak of the 'Word of God' which is the real creative power, the all-permeative source of the energy that has brought the universe into being.

This is true of our physical bodies, as well as of the air, and all the material objects that surround us, and because of this we are with and within God every moment of our lives. He is not far away. Wherever else He may be, He is always here, with and within each of us. God is all in all and no one can be apart from God. There is no separation from Him at any time.

Actually, solid matter as such does not exist. For if everything is composed of energy, where then is solid matter? Today's scientists have shown us that such seemingly solid things as tables and chairs, or giant skyscrapers of steel and stone, are basically composed of atoms that contain empty space and energy in the form of electrical discharges. But the scientists have not yet shown us that the source of this energy is the Word or Holy Spirit of the Supreme Creator and Father, the same all-powerful Father mentioned so often by the beloved Master Jesus during his ministry on earth.

In addition to the Christian Bible, the scriptures of the other major religions also state that the Word is the Creator and sustainer of the universe. The Hindu Vedas say that the fourteen parts of the world were created by 'Nad' or the Divine Word; and the Holy Koran says that 'Kalma' or the Word of God created the universe. The Indian Masters have spoken many times of the Word as the creator and sustainer.

Thus Guru Nanak says:

> 'From Shabd (the Word) is the earth, from Shabd is the sky,
> from Shabd emanateth all light. The whole creation resteth
> on Shabd and this Shabd, O Nanak, abideth in us all.'

'Creation, Dissolution and Re-creation is done by Shabd.'

In the *Adi Granth* it is written:

> 'Shabd createth, Shabd dissolveth; and Shabd again bringeth
> Creation into being.'

> 'Nam (the Word) supporteth all worlds and universes.'

Shams-i-Tabriz pointed out the same truth when he said:

> 'This Sound (or Word) createth the whole universe, and to
> all lights giveth it birth.'

The great twentieth century Master, Sawan Singh Ji, of
Beas, Punjab, speaking of the same subject, says:

> 'The Word is the foundation on which the whole visible and
> invisible structure of the universe is resting. Everything has
> sprung from this Word . . . the Word has been, now is, and
> always will be the Basic Reality.'

And the Master Jesus, stressing that the Word is
imperishable and from everlasting unto everlasting, said:

> 'Heaven and earth shall pass away, but my words (the
> Word) shall not pass away.'
>
>   *Matthew 24 : 35*

The Life of All

The Word is also our own life-force, for all life comes
from it. It is the very essence and being of all things,
ourselves included, the life of all that lives. There is not a
living creature in all the material worlds that does not derive
its life and energy from this life current. For God is life,

intelligent life-force, and without Him, nothing could live for a single moment, or even exist. God, manifested in the Holy Spirit, is the only life, exactly as the sap is the true life of the tree. The life-force of the Word exists in and maintains all human beings, good or bad, rich or poor, saints or sinners, men, women, and children. No human being is without it.

Says Guru Nanak:

'This Shabad, O Nanak, abideth in us all.'

Jesus, speaking of the Word as the life of all created beings, also as the spiritual life inherent in all men, said:

'It is the spirit (Holy Spirit or Word) that quickeneth; the flesh profiteth nothing; the words that I speak unto you, they are spirit, and they are life.'

John 6 : 63

There seems little doubt that the actual message given by Jesus was:

'The Word of which I speak unto you, it is spirit, and it is life.'

Thus the love and life and power of God which brought the universe into being is our own real life, the inner spiritual energy that sustains the outer form. This current of divine life-force flows continuously into every electron in every atom of every person's body. It flows through the human nervous system as a current of light, which is imperceptible to the physical eyes because of its high rate of vibration. It is the Word or Holy Spirit which really gives life to our bodies and sustains them. Without its invisible presence our bodies and those of all living creatures would immediately stop functioning and become inert pieces of matter.

The Supreme Being is the beating of our hearts, and the blood that pulses through our veins. He is our breathing, and the air we breathe.

Thus God dwells within us and is our very life. He is so near that he hears our feeblest whisper, aye, even before we speak. It was this truth that inspired Tennyson when he wrote:

'Speak to him, thou, for He heareth
And spirit to spirit can speak.
Nearer is He than breathing,
Closer than hands and feet.'

And Tennyson again expressed this basic truth in the lines:

'If thou wouldst hear the Nameless, and wilt dive
Into the Temple-cave of thine own self,
There, brooding by the central altar, thou
Mayst haply learn the Nameless hath a voice,
By which thou wilt abide, if thou be wise.'

We are as close to God as we ever shall be. All that is needed is to know this by experiment and experience. And this is made abundantly possible for all who follow the path of the Masters.

The ultimate purpose of human life is to find this life or Holy Spirit of God, to realise it, and to be borne upward by it to our original home. This was pointed out by Guru Nanak when he said:

'The object of thy coming into the world is to possess the treasure house of inestimable riches, the Elixir of Life, which blesses you with immortal existence. This Nectar of Life (The Word or Holy Spirit) thou canst drink only through the grace of the Master.'

When the time comes, man will find that in the mysterious depth of his own being there reside the life and love, and the wisdom, power, and peace of God. In short, the Divine Word of God.

CHAPTER 5

THE WIND BLOWETH

'The wind bloweth where it listeth, and thou hearest the sound thereof, but canst not tell whence it cometh, and whither it goeth; so is every one that is born of the Spirit.'

— John 3 : 8

'And the word which ye hear is not mine, but the Father's which sent me.'

— John 14 : 24

At first glance there may seem to be no connection between the two quotations given above. Both statements, however, refer to the same great truth—the Word of God, which in essence is the mighty outpouring stream of boundless love, life, and power emanating without ceasing from the Supreme Creator of the universe.

The Word of God is, and always has been the most important factor in the teaching of the Masters—of the teachings of Jesus as well as of the Masters of today. It is mentioned under different names in the scriptures of all the great world religions, though its meaning has been known to but few of the followers of these religions.

The Hindu scriptures call it Anahat Shabd, or the Unstruck Music, and also Akash Bani, the Celestial Voice. Mohammedans call it Kalma, or Word, and Kalam-i-Ilahi, or Voice of God. Zoroaster speaks of it as Sraosha, meaning 'the Sound from the Sky.' The early Greek philosophers who had learned the spiritual secrets of India, refer to it as the

Logos, while some called it the music of the spheres. Socrates speaks of it as an inner sound that transported him to realms of transcendent and divine beauty.

The Masters of today call it Nam, meaning Name or Word (of God); and also Shabd (pronounced Shubud), which means Sound, or more particularly, spiritual Sound. In the English language the Word is called the Sound Current or the Audible Life Stream.

These names are given to it because the Word, which is God in dynamic action, can be heard by human beings whose inner ear has been opened by a perfect Master. The ability to hear the Sound Current is given by the Master to each disciple at the time of initiation.

The light of the current of the Word can also be seen by a Master's disciples. For the primal manifestations of the Supreme Father to human beings appear in the form of inner light and sound, both of which are inherent in and emanate from the Sound Current.

The fact that the Word is audible is one of the most vital of all facts to the disciple. For when he hears the sacred and sublime music of the Sound Current, he hears God Himself. The Audible Life Stream is, as the Masters have pointed out, God's 'unspoken language', and His 'unwritten Word'.

The term Sound Current is new to most western readers, and because of this fact, its identity with familiar terms used in the Bible must be made abundantly clear. The Sound Current is the Holy Spirit or Holy Ghost of the Bible and is the same thing as 'the Word' spoken of by St. John. In all of the Bible, wherever the terms Holy Spirit or Holy Ghost are used, they refer to the Sound Current or the Word. In this book also, the terms are used interchangeably.

The Holy Trinity of the Church, the Father, the Son and the Holy Ghost, is the Trinity of the Supreme Father, the living Master, and the Sound Current—Word of God, or Holy

Spirit. Thus, to become 'filled with the Holy Spirit' is to hear and participate in the Audible Life Stream, to become absorbed in it and become one with it or one with God. A realisation of this fact gives one a better understanding of the meaning and real nature of the Holy Trinity, which is so often spoken of in the doctrine of the Christian Church.

Vibrating and resounding without ceasing throughout all the illimitable reaches of space, and also within each atom and each human being, the heavenly strains of the Sound Current are heard by the Masters and their disciples in the form of indescribably enchanting music. The ethereal beauty of this music, moreover, exerts an irresistible magnetic power that draws the disciple upwards and leads him stage by stage through all the many mansions of his Father's house until, safe at last, he reaches his eternal home in the highest of the heavens.

This, in briefest outline, is the method of salvation decreed since time immemorial by the Supreme Creator God. The Word, together with all its spiritual power to draw us upward to a far higher, better and happier life is resounding every moment within each and every human life. It needs only the help of the living Master to be able to hear its melodies.

'The wind bloweth . . . and thou hearest the sound thereof' is the most specific description of the celestial voice of God, made by Jesus. His reference to hearing is recognised by the eastern Masters as ample evidence that he was speaking of the Sound Current—the eternal music of the Word of God.

Confirmation of this fact is given by the Master Sawan Singh, who says:

> 'From the Bible we learn that Christ did follow the Sound Current. Even now, if you go within, you meet him on the way. To understand Christ and his science, let us go within and meet him.'
>
> *Spiritual Gems, letter No. 144*

There are many other statements attributed to Jesus in which he probably referred to the fact that the Word is audible and can be heard by those for whom the Way has been opened. These statements were later interpreted by translators and others who did not know the truth, and were worded to indicate that Jesus was referring to his spoken words, his outer teaching. But in each case there seems little doubt that he spoke of the 'unspoken Word', the Sound Current. The following are a few examples:

> 'Why do ye not understand my speech? Even because ye cannot hear my word (Word).'
>
> *John 8 : 43*

> 'He that is of God heareth God's words: ye therefore hear them not, because ye are not of God.' (He that is of God heareth God's Word: ye therefore hear it not, because ye are not of God.),'
>
> *John 8 : 47*

> 'The words that I speak unto you, they are spirit, and they are life.' (The Word of which I speak unto you, it is spirit, and it is life.)
>
> *John 6 : 63*

The Masters of the east have spoken of the wonderful sound of the Holy Spirit over and over again:

> 'A Sound is vibrating in the whole of creation. When you open your inner ear you will hear a continuous Sound which will lead you across all limitations of mind and matter. My Beloved is speaking to you all the time. Alas! You do not hear His Voice.'
>
> *Shah Niaz*

> 'Bring the Firmament under thy feet, O thou brave man, and listen thou to the melodious Song coming from the heavens above.'
>
> *Maulana Rum*

'Anahad Shabad has no figure, no form;
It is the sound from the Immaculate one.'

Guru Nanak

Whoever finds a genuine Master and devotes himself to the simple spiritual practices that he teaches will contact the Holy Spirit and in so doing will hear the Word of God. This is the first step on the spiritual path, and it is one of the demonstrated facts of the spiritual science of the Masters. It is not theory. It is a fact proven by personal experience and demonstration, which has been verified over and over again by many thousands of disciples. Every initiated disciple can prove it for himself, if he devotes himself to the practice. He cannot fail, if he does the work.

The most important facts that should be understood about the Sound Current are that it is God Himself and that it is now within every human being. It is the Supreme Creator, manifested and manifesting. It is not only an emanation of God, but it is God Himself. God is not static. He is superlatively dynamic, and the Sound Current is His dynamic energy and intelligent life-force in a continuous process of manifestation. It is the omnipresent form of God, which flows into and through everything from the highest to the lowest, and surrounds and pervades everything in the universe.

'The Audible Life Stream is the everlasting form of the Lord, and is always within every one of us,' says the Master Sawan Singh.

But while the Holy Word is within each one of us, we cannot hear its melodies or see its light because we are spiritually deaf and blind. It is to this fact that Jesus referred when he said: 'Ye have eyes and ye see not, and ye have ears and ye hear not.' It is only after acceptance and training by a living perfect Master that our inner ears and eyes are opened and we can at last become aware of the radiant divinity within us.

Without Sat Guru (a living perfect Master) none can get Nam (the Word or Sound Current),' says the *Adi Granth*. 'The Lord Himself hath thus designed the universe.'

And in all probability it was this fact that Jesus brought out when he told his disciples:

> 'Unto you it is given to know the mystery of the kingdom of God . . . The sower (the Master) soweth the word.'
>
> *Mark : 4 : 14*

Down through the centuries, over and over again, in all ages, men have asked: How can we know God? To be sure, He can be known indirectly by inference in many ways, as through the laws of nature or the tenderness of human love. But this is not enough.

To virtually all men, God is still no more than an abstract idea, a mental concept. What is needed is to convert this mental concept into something that is real to human experience. And this can be done only by enabling the human individual to see and hear God, for personal sight and hearing are necessary before anything or anybody can become real to human beings.

Is this possible? The answer of the Masters is an unqualified yes. God can be known directly by seeing His light within us and by hearing within ourselves the soul-absorbing melodies of His Word, the Sound Current.

Pleading with mortals to recognise these facts and enter upon the Path of Light, Maulana Rum urges:

> 'O seek thou that Music which never dieth;
> O find thou that Sun that never setteth.'

That Sun, the radiant light of the Audible Life Stream, is visible only to those whose inner eyes have been opened by the Master; and that music is audible to those alone for whom the Master has opened the inner ear. The world at large is

unaware of the transcendent beauty of these manifestations
of God's Being. It is only the Masters and their disciples who
hear that heavenly harmony and behold that celestial light.
Says Shams-i-Tabriz:

> 'We should see God with our own inner eye and hear His
> voice with our inner ear. We should penetrate the dark veil
> within and behold His glory.'

This, the living Master enables us to do.

God Himself, in essence, is formless. He cannot be described
in mortal language, because no language in this world contains
the thought-forms, ideas, or concepts that are needed to
describe Him. Man, while earth-bound, is too limited in
comprehension to be able to realise His infinite majesty and
glory. But God in action as the mighty life stream of the
Sound Current is a vibratory force pervading every atom in
the universe and manifesting in the form of light and sound.
When a living Master has opened the disciple's inner eye and
ear, he may then know God directly by seeing His light and
hearing His Word or Sound.
Says Shah Niaz:

> 'The whole universe is full of this Voice, if you can but
> open your (inner) ear and listen to it.'

This celestial voice is the all-powerful Father reaching
down to the individual man to give illumination and spiritual
power, and finally to lead him to his eternal home, after it has
purified and fitted him for that abode.
It is the link between man and God.
Listening with reverence and devotion to this Voice of
God and becoming absorbed in it is true worship. It has long
been clear to theologians, as well as to many others, that God
does not demand worship because He needs it or desires it,

but because it is the means whereby the soul of man can return to the source from which it came. True worship is the state or condition in which man stands humbly in the presence of his Creator. It is the recognition or awareness that there is an immense power that is greater than all other powers, and that this power is benevolent and helpful towards all creatures, including man. When one can hear the voice of God within himself, and feel its spiritualising power, he stands in the presence of his Creator and is truly worshipping.

The love, life, and power of God made manifest and dynamic in the tremendous spiritual force of the Sound Current is the supreme and basic fact of the entire universe; and it is also the central and most important factor in the spiritual science of the Masters. It is the very foundation of their system, and it is the factor that distinguishes their method of spiritual growth and liberation from all other present-day religions, spiritual or occult systems, as well as from the usual systems of Yoga taught in India.

It should not be forgotten, moreover, that the method of the Masters is the method established and ordained by the Supreme Creator Himself for the redemption and salvation of all true spiritual seekers.

The knowledge, practice, and teaching of the Sound Current is the one unmistakable sign by which a perfect Master may be known and recognized from among all others. For no one is or can be a spiritual Master of the highest order with the power to liberate or 'save' all who come to him unless he teaches and gives to his disciples the gift of the Sound Current or the Holy Spirit.

Says Guru Arjan Dev:

> 'Accept him alone as a Master who can make thee embedded in Truth, makes thee realise the unfathomable, and unites thee with the Sound Current.'

'The Sat Guru (True Master) is he who has it in his power
to give us union with the Infinite while we are in our finite
bodies.'

And Soami Ji of Agra emphasised this truth when he said:

'Who giveth thee knowledge of Shabd (the Word), he is a
perfect Guru. Become thou the dust of his feet.'

Like the wind of which Jesus spoke, the Sound Current is
not visible to the eye of the physical body. We see the wind's
results, we feel its power, and we hear it, but it remains ever
an unseen force. So it is with the Sound Current, which is the
spiritual life and energy of God and the voice of the Supreme
Creator.

When one hears it with his own inner ear, his life is
transformed, for this experience brings a knowledge of God's
presence that creates implicit trust. This trust is unshakable,
because it is based upon direct experience that cannot be
denied. It is as St. Paul says, who could himself see the inner
light and hear the inner sound:

'Faith cometh by hearing, and hearing by the word (Word)
of God.'

Romans 10 : 17

And in this way, by creating an unwavering faith in God
and His indwelling presence, the Word restores religion to its
rightful place as the most important factor in the life of an
individual. For when there is an utter trust in God based upon
indisputable personal experience, religion, or the spiritual
quest, becomes the supreme human concern, the one and
only pursuit that can give to life real purpose, worth, and
meaning.

CHAPTER 6

I AND MY FATHER ARE ONE

'I and my Father are one.'

—*John 10 : 30*

'He that hath seen me hath seen the Father.'
—*John 14 : 9*

'The Father is in me, and I in him.'
—*John 10 : 38*

Many Christians accept without question the fact that Jesus was the son of God and one with the Father. His sayings, such as those cited above, are taken as literal statements of fact. And, indeed, that is exactly what they are.

Among spiritually minded persons in the eastern countries Jesus is also revered as a veritable Son of the Father. But, as has already been pointed out, there is a striking difference between their viewpoint and that of many western Christians. To the eastern peoples, Jesus is but one of the many beloved and special children of God who have been sent to this earth from the higher realms.

In the eyes of eastern peoples the perfect Masters of all ages, and of the present day as well, are the sons of God, as was Jesus, sent here by the Supreme Father to do his work.

It is noteworthy that the sayings of the eastern Masters, made with all the humility and love which characterise each and everyone of these great light-bearers, bring out over and over again the fact stated above by Jesus, that all perfect Masters are one with the Father and are His beloved sons.

'The Masters are the children of God,' says Maulana Rum. 'When they are in His presence and when they are absent, ever are they under His eyes.'

In the *Adi Granth* it is said:

'The Father and the Son are dyed in the same colour.'

And Guru Nanak declares:

'The Steward of God becomes God Himself;
Do not be deceived by His human body.'

Not only are the perfect Masters the sons of God; they are also one with God.

All of them are one with the Father, and whoever sees a living perfect Master of today sees the Father just as certainly as did the followers of Jesus.

Jesus stated this truth very explicitly in his reply to the disciple Philip, who said: 'Lord, show us the Father, and it sufficeth us.'

To this Jesus answered:

'Have I been so long time with you, and yet hast thou not known me, Philip? He that hath seen me hath seen the Father, and how sayest thou, then, "Shew us the Father?" Believest thou not that I am in the Father, and the Father in me? the words that I speak unto you I speak not of myself; but the Father that dwelleth in me, he doeth the works. Believe me that I am in the Father, and the Father in me.'

John 14 : 9-11

In their individual ways the eastern Masters have many times expressed this same fundamental truth:

'Now I am One with Thee, and beholding this Oneness, is my mind pacified . . . God hath put Himself in the Guru.
'Under thy shelter have I come, O Master; one with the powerful and merciful God art thou.'

Guru Nanak

'God and Kabir have become One, and none can distinguish betwixt the two.'

Kabir Sahib

'Be it known too that the Inner Secret is known only to a Sant Sat Guru or to one to whom He has revealed it. The Sant Sat Guru does not depend upon discourses or teachings or scriptures. He Himself is the Supreme Being in human form.'

Soami Ji Maharaj

'The Greatness of the Master is indescribable. He is the fountainhead of the Elixir of Life (the Sound Current). He was before the Creation and before the beginning of each cycle of time. He is God Himself.'

Guru Arjan Dev

'God and his Masters are one, of this have thou no doubt. One they are, as the wave riseth above the water and mergeth into it again.

'Guru-who is God, do thou worship with all thy heart and soul; for giveth He life, and sustaineth He all.'

Adi Granth

'God cometh in the form of man (The Master); and cometh He to awaken the world.'

Bulleh Shah

Shams-i-Tabriz expresses this truth in a particularly interesting manner. He says:

'That Great Lord (the Supreme Father) hath put Himself behind fast-closed doors (beyond the reach of the intellect or senses). Then, concealed in the cloak of man, (the Master), cometh He to open the door.'

Within the Master, God is hidden.

A perfect Master and the Supreme Being Himself are the same, with the sole difference that the Master has assumed a human body and is to some extent limited by that body. Spiritually, the Master has no limitations whatever. His inner being is one with the Supreme Being who created and governs the universe.

'If seekest thou union with God, O sit thou at the holy feet of the Masters,' says Maulana Rum. 'A few moments of their company are better than a hundred years of sincere prayer. Inside the Masters is the mosque, and there is God for thy homage and worship.'

The great Saint Soami Ji of Agra, writes in the *Sar Bachan:*

> 'The human form of the perfect Master is for the purpose of making Himself known. His real form is one with that of the Lord, as He is always enjoying the bliss of the Holy Presence of Sat Purush.'

The Supreme Lord God is infinite and cannot be seen with the physical eyes. But He is focused or localised in His Saints and Masters, and can be seen and known by seeing and knowing them. From these facts it is possible to obtain a clearer idea of the immensity of a perfect Master's powers. He is, without question, the greatest among men. While he appears to his disciples as a gentle, humble, and loving friend and human being, his spiritual powers are virtually unlimited. The Master leaves his physical body at will and in an instant is in Sat Desh. He is at home in all the regions of the grand divisions of the universe.

In India the perfect Masters are frequently referred to as Saints, the word being taken from the Sanskrit word Sant, which has the same meaning. But it should be pointed out that this has no reference to canonical saints, like those of the church. It refers strictly and solely to a great soul who has developed his latent spiritual powers, risen to oneness with the Supreme Creator and is now able to conduct his disciples to the same sublime achievement[1].

---

1. All perfect Masters are Saints, but all Saints (those who have reached the highest realm) are not Masters. Perfect Mastership is conferred on a disciple only by a perfect living Master.

Such a Saint is called in India, a Sant Sat Guru, a term which is used at times throughout this book. Literally it means a Saint who is a true spiritual teacher and guide, than whom there is no higher.

Since all perfect Masters are sons of God and one with God it follows that this is true of the living perfect Masters of today. If we want God, we should seek Him there; and if we want to worship God, we should worship Him in them. There is no other living form of God in this world than the person of the perfect Master and consequently God cannot be worshipped *directly* here in any other way than by worshipping the Master.

To millions in the east, older and wiser perhaps than we, this method of worshipping God, so alien to the millions of the west, is the only true, logical, and rational method. Dr Julian P. Johnson speaks of it eloquently in his book, *With a Great Master in India:*

'This writer has frequently watched the crowds thronging the Master, many of them men and women of culture, offering some of the most phenomenal demonstrations of devotion. He has many times tried to analyse it into its psychological elements. Often with tears in their eyes, hands folded in an attitude of worship, and on their faces the radiance of joy and love. There is nothing else like it to be found on earth.

'Nowhere has he witnessed such beautiful, spontaneous, and joyous worship as that given to the Master, the beloved Sat Guru. In their faces, thousands of them in one great throng, they show combined love and joy and cheerful realisation. Sometimes accentuated by tears of gladness, their eyes sparkle as if lit up by the light of the third heaven. Here is worship with perfect understanding mingled with love.

'They know exactly whom and what they are worshipping. It is no theological belief with them. Their living Lord is right there before their eyes, and he is not a theory. To these people the Master is all there is, God of Heaven and of eternal life, combined and embodied in this human form. The most astute and analytical philosophers among them see nothing inconsistent in the idea of God and man being fully expressed in one form right among them. To them it is in fact the normal thing, and they cannot imagine the full expression of divine love on earth in any other manner.

'When they have seen the Master, and learnt to love him, they know that they can depend upon him for eternal life. They know in their souls that seeing him now, today, they have that boundless life already. It is not a far away hope, a vague intangible something to be wondered about. It is a present possession. And so why shouldn't they be filled with joy?

'It would be idle to call this blind devotion. That would be an unfortunate reflection upon the intelligence and fair-mindedness of the person making such a comment. If you could witness such devotion yourself, you would know that it is the intelligent worship of the soul. The worship of the Master is a living joy, unlike anything else on earth.

'In the Master's presence it is all light. No shadow can remain and it carries with it its own internal evidence of truth and reality. Borne up upon this reality, the heart takes wings like an eagle. And yet probably nothing else but a personal experience ever would have convinced this disciple of that sublime reality. He does not expect everyone else to accept it all at once.'

It is true that all men have oneness with the Supreme Father—our souls are drops in the boundless ocean of His Being. But ordinary men are not conscious of their divine inner nature. They have lost their awareness of this unity. The Master, on the other hand, is always conscious of it. That is one of the qualities that distinguishes him from ordinary men. The Master knows his relationship with the Father, and is able consciously to exercise his powers as a son of God.

And the Master is the Lord Himself. For the infinite creator is universal spirit. He becomes dynamic in the Masters, and thus sheds His holy radiance among men. The Master manifests the Lord; but he does not manifest all of the Lord in this one human body.

Likewise, the ordinary man is a spark of the divine essence; but he has not yet developed into that glowing, radiant light that the Master has become.

The truth that the genuine Masters are sons of God and one with God does not have to be accepted by faith alone. Like all other statements made in connection with the spiritual science of the Masters, it can be fully proved and demonstrated to be true. When the disciples of a living Master rise up into the higher spheres, they are able to meet the Master there, see his inner radiant or astral form with their own eyes, and know from their own experience that the Master and God are one.

But here on earth, where we can see only gross matter, it is as Maulana Rum says:

'The sun is hidden behind the human curtain (the body).'

The Real Form of the Masters

There is, in addition, a special way in which the Masters are one with the Supreme Creator. This is the fact that the inner being of every perfect Master is the Word or Holy spirit of God, the Audible Life Stream. His true essence is the divine Sound Current, which is God's life, love, and power in action.

Speaking of this truth, one of the Masters says:

'Saints and Masters appear outwardly like ordinary human beings, but in their inner selves they are connected with Shabd or the Audible Life Stream, nay, they are Shabd incarnate. There is no difference between Saints and Shabd or God. God is the sea and Saints are its waves. The waves rise out of the sea, live on it, and are finally merged into it. Similarly, Saints are born out of Shabd, take up the body, and teach the wisdom of Shabd to men, and finally go back and merge into Shabd. They unite us back to Shabd, and so we love them. They make us like themselves, raise us to the same spiritual height which they have attained.'

Jesus stated this same truth when he told the disciples:

'I came forth from the Father, and am come into the word: again, I leave the world, and go to the Father.'

John 16 : 28

And the Bible speaks of the immanence of the Word in the Master Jesus in the passage that says:

'And Jesus being full of the Holy Ghost (the Word) returned from Jordan.'

Luke 4 : 1

Again, the Bible says:

'And the Word was made flesh, and dwelt among us.'

John 1 : 14

The identical truth is given in the *Adi Granth*, which says:

'Shabd (the Sound Current) is Guru, and soul is the disciple of this Melody.'

Master Sawan Singh Ji of Beas also speaks of this truth, saying:

'The real form of the Master is the Word. It is present everywhere and is the mainstay of all that is, visible and invisible. The Word takes the human form to connect people with Himself, for people would not understand in any other way except through someone like themselves. St. John says the Word was made flesh and dwelt among us.'

There is an inspiring concept associated with the fact that the Master is one with the Supreme. This is that every man is a potential Saint, and is therefore potentially identical with God. He needs only development and realisation. To become one with the Father is the supreme goal of all human evolution, and the sole object of our being here on earth is that we may grow to the spiritual stature of the Masters, who are the true supermen.

> 'Be ye therefore perfect, even as your Father which is in Heaven is perfect.'
>
> *Matthew 5 : 48*

Men only require a living Master to help them to develop and reach this goal. They need but the light of Mastership in another man to kindle the light within themselves.

The Master's Love

Being at one with God, the Masters partake of all His qualities, and of these the greatest is divine love. Above all other things, the Masters are the love of God incarnate. God is love—a boundless ocean of love and mercy—and the Masters, being one with God, are in like manner infinite in their love for their disciples and for all mankind. Their love passeth all understanding, and is beyond all bounds.

> 'God is love; and he that dwelleth in love dwelleth in God, and God in him.'
>
> *1 John 4 : 16*

In an effort to express this fact in a manner that can be easily grasped by the ordinary human mind, the Indian scriptures say that the love of a Master for his disciples is a thousand times as great as the love of a mother for her child. He is the embodiment of the infinite and divine love of God.

To the disciples of a perfect Master, the words of one of

the favourite Christian hymns have a very special meaning, expressing as they do the boundless love of the Master:

'I know not where His islands lift
Their fronded palms in air;
I only know I cannot drift
Beyond His Love and Care.'

And the words of the Psalmist carry the same message to one who has come under the protection of a true Master:

'If I take the wings of the morning, and dwell in the uttermost parts of the sea; even there shall thy hand lead me, and thy right hand shall hold me.'

Psalms 139 : 9

The love of a perfect Master for his disciples is so great that the ordinary human being finds it difficult or even impossible to comprehend it. It is only as a disciple makes some progress on the path that the real truth and meaning of the Master's perfect and neverfailing love slowly becomes apparent and the disciple's being becomes flooded with gratefulness and thanks for such a priceless gift.

Over and over again the eastern Masters have tried to express in words the abiding love of the Masters for all whom they have taken into their fold and are leading to their heavenly home.

Guru Nanak says:

'As the Mother, giving birth to a son, brings him up, keeping her eye on him within doors and without, putting morsels into his mouth, fondling him every moment, in the same manner does the Sat Guru keep his disciple with love and endearment.'

Bu Ali describes the love of God which flows through the Master by saying:

'Of the grace of God thou knowest not, for every moment
like a lover doth He be hold thee.'
'If of His love didst thou know, then wouldst thou find that
keener is He than thyself.'

The disciple knows, after he has progressed a little distance
on the path, that he has no other such friend and well-wisher
in all the world as his beloved Master, either here or hereafter.
It is as Soami Ji of Agra says:

'Only a perfect Master and the Word are your two real
friends. Give your heart to them and throw out all else
from it.'

The soul loves God intensely, but God, and the Master
who is His son, love the soul even more intensely.

CHAPTER 7

I AM THE WAY

'I am the Way, the Truth, and the Life: no man cometh unto the Father, but by me.'
—John 14 : 6

In the days when Jesus gave his message to mankind, he was able to show his followers the Way that leads to the true home. In his statement given above, he speaks of this fact. But he does not say, it may be noted, that he would or could take new disciples to the Father after his departure from the earth.

During the centuries that followed Jesus' departure his words were often misconstrued and in the end the church formulated the doctrine that no one could return to the higher realms except by the aid of Jesus himself. All other Masters were ignored and in effect banned.

It has already been pointed out that there have been many more great spiritual Masters, all of whom were the Way to eternal life, than the few known to most people in the west. This fact is here emphasized again and further elaborated, because it is of such supreme importance to the people of today.

That the western people do not know of the unbroken succession of Masters who have blessed the world with their holy presence throughout the centuries is only natural, for most of them have been taught since childhood that Jesus was the only son of God to dwell on earth. But there have been many others, and if any reader is in doubt on this point, let him study the records and the scriptures of the Masters and

Saints of the east, particularly India and Persia. In them he may discover new facts that will widen his horizon and alter his previously held ideas.

The western viewpoint may be partly or largely due to the statement in the Gospel according to St John, which says:

'God so loved the world that he gave his only begotten Son.'
John 3 : 16

This view, to put the matter plainly, simply does not coincide with the facts of history as they are and have been known to millions living in other parts of the world during thousands of years.

Another familiar statement in the Bible has also contributed to the western belief that Jesus was the only Master in the long history of the world. This is Jesus' own statement:

'For one is your Master, even Christ.'
Matthew 23 : 10

Commenting on this statement, Master Sawan Singh says:

'Every Saint has said the same. The Word is the latent 'Christ' in all. People are in darkness and do not comprehend that they are the Word in and out—flesh light, life. If they could comprehend the Word in themselves they would be in light and alive and in the Kingdom of God in Heaven. Jesus was Christ on account of his comprehension of the Word in Him, and thereby he had arisen above the weakness of the flesh and was capable of lifting others to his level.'
Spiritual Gems, letter No. 105

Among the great spiritual Masters of the past were several who lived and taught at the same time as the Renaissance period in Europe, from the thirteenth to the sixteenth century. There was a widespread spiritual awakening in India at that time under the guidance of Guru Nanak, Kabir Sahib, the poet weaver of Benares, and many other great and widely known Masters. In Persia, some time earlier, a similar spiritual revival took place under the leadership of Maulana Rum and Shams-i-Tabriz. Another Persian Master whose influence is still strongly felt today was the great fourteenth-century Master, Hafiz. Some of the many other noted Indian Masters whose names are still widely known and venerated include Baba Farid, Bulleh Shah, Dadu Ji, Paltu Sahib, Jagjiwan Sahib, Nabha Ji, Soami Ji, Baba Jaimal Singh, Sawan Singh Ji Maharaj, Sardar Bahadur Jagat Singh and Maharaj Charan Singh Ji of Beas. There have been many others.

The work of all these Masters during their lifetimes on earth always has been, and is today, to initiate those who are seeking for the path, and to help them to follow the path. This, also, was one part of the mission of Jesus. But after he departed from this earth, his work of initiating and guiding new disciples came to an end. This is not to say that he does not still play a part in the divine plan for this world. It simply means that his work on earth of starting new disciples on the path to their true home is finished.

There are other passages in the New Testament in which Jesus clearly indicates that his mission of teaching the truth and initiating those who were ready was to be done during his short life in the material body. In the following quotations the words in parentheses are added to aid in making this meaning clear:

In John 9 : 4-5 Jesus says:

> 'I must work the works of him that sent me, while it is day (during my lifetime): the night cometh when no man can work. (Only) as long as I am in the world, I am the light of the world.'

And again, in John 12:35-6, there is the statement:

> 'Yet a little while (until I leave you) is the light with you. Walk while ye have the light, lest (spiritual) darkness come upon you: for he that walketh in darkness knoweth not

whither he goeth. While ye have light (while I am with
you), believe in the light, that ye may be the children of
light.'

In the east, it is widely known that when the earth life of
a Master ends, the specific work the Supreme Father sent him
to do is also finished.

The real work of each Master on this earth plane lasts only
during his lifetime here in a human body, and ends with the
end of that human lifetime. The Master assumes human form
in order to do a particular work which he could not do
without that form. This work is to initiate and guide the
seekers who are ready for the spiritual path at the time that
the Master is on earth.

When the earth life of a Master ends, his work on the earth
is finished, just as the work on earth of anyone else is
completed. The Master continues to guide his disciples from
the higher realms. But he does not initiate more disciples.
That work is carried on by his successors.

In the east, this fact is often driven home by pointing out
that no one today can obtain medicine from a doctor who
lived and died a thousand years or more ago. Nor can one
retain the services of a lawyer of ancient Greece or Rome to
decide a present-day case. Hannibal and Caesar, great generals
though they were, cannot today lead armies into battle.

Both doctor and lawyer, both Hannibal and Caesar, finished
their particular and specialised work on this earth when they
departed from it. Exactly the same holds true in the case of
the great spiritual Masters. It is not possible for a Master who
left this earth many years ago to initiate present-day disciples
and give them the training and guidance they need to make
steady progress on the spiritual path. This is true, not because
the Masters' powers are limited but because human beings
are limited. The Master has all the powers of the Supreme
Father, at whose behest and as whose agent in the divine plan

he comes to this earth.

For a Master to contact us, however, and talk with us and teach us, he must assume human form. We cannot receive what he wishes to give unless he is in a human body, and can therefore communicate with us. The living Masters who now carry on the Father's work are the modern Christs, the elder brothers and saviours of mankind.

In administering the affairs of the universe the Supreme Lord God directs His power down to lower worlds through the rulers of the different regions by means of His Word or current of almighty power. Each ruler in his own sphere is the centre for the distribution of the Word's creative and sustaining life forces. All of them carry on their work in accordance with the will of the Supreme One.

The exponent of His Word through whom His infinite power flows on this earth, is the Sat Guru or perfect Master. He carries on his work under the orders of the Supreme One Himself. The Masters are His ambassadors and executive officers on earth, and they have a unique and special duty. This is to show the Way to those who are ready, to rescue them from the bondage and darkness of this world and take them up to the spiritual liberty and light of the highest spiritual regions. This is their chief duty and it is assigned to them because there is no other way by which the souls imprisoned in human bodies can escape from the wilderness of this world, journey upward through the many mansions of the Father's house, and return at last to their true home.

There are true Masters living in the world today, and those who search for them in right earnest will find them. This fact is emphasized and re-emphasized here simply because it is a new idea to so many in the west, and among those many there may be some who will chance upon this book and find in it the confirmation of the Master's presence for which they have been seeking.

'Do you imagine that God showed Himself to man only in those far-off days when Christ stirred up an obscure corner of the Roman Empire or when Buddha walked with the begging-bowl?' says Paul Brunton in his discerning book, *The Secret Path*. 'If God cannot show Himself again today, then His power has become strangely circumscribed and the absolute has suddenly shrunk back to the finite. Is it not better to believe that He is ready to reveal Himself to all who care to fulfil the conditions precedent to revelation? The Eternal has spoken to man in the past and can speak to him again.'

Many in the west, when they are first told of the need for a living Master ask the question: why, since God is everywhere present and is all-powerful, is it necessary to have the aid of a living Master in order to find Him?

This is a very logical question, and it requires a definite and clearcut answer. The answer, as given by the Masters, is that the supreme Father has ordained this method as part of His divine Plan for the redemption and salvation of those who live in the material worlds. A human being is too limited to contact God directly. For this purpose a human being needs communication with and instruction from another human being who is simultaneously at our level and at the same level as the Supreme Father. Such communication is obviously possible only with a living Master. It is a law, therefore, made by the Supreme Father Himself that there must be a human contact, albeit a highly spiritualised one, through which the Creator can contact those who are ready and eager to set their feet on the true path of spiritual progress. This human contact is the living Master, and the Master is the most important factor in the Supreme Father's plan of salvation. It is as Jesus says:

'No man cometh unto the Father, but by me.'

John 14 : 6

When Jesus made this statement, it was true of him and of his time, for he was then a living Master. But through the years these words have been misinterpreted, so that many today believe that Jesus is still the only person able to bring souls to the Father. Had Jesus meant that, he would not have said 'As long as I am in the world, I am the light of the world,' or made the other observations cited earlier. A living Master is needed, just as he was needed in the time of Jesus' life on earth. And in this connection, it must be remembered that the Masters' love and reverence for Jesus and their comprehension of his earthly mission are far greater than our own.

God Himself, in His immaterial form, does not talk directly to human beings. He does not as a rule teach them patiently day after day and answer their numberless questions in a way that will entirely satisfy their intellects. To do these things, man, being constituted as he is, needs another human being.

In the Adi Granth the living Master of that day said, precisely as did Jesus :

> 'I have come to take you back to Him who sent you into the world.'

And the Master Soami Ji of Agra says in the *Sar Bachan:*

> 'The human form of the Sant Sat Guru is for the purpose of contact with mankind. His real form is One with that of the Lord, as he is always enjoying the bliss of the Supreme Father.'

The greatness of a genuine Master cannot be understood or evaluated, however, by the limited human intelligence which can see only the human form. For the Masters have divine powers that are far beyond the human ken. Spiritually, they have no limitations whatever, any more than God himself has any limitations. Inwardly, the Masters are one with the universal Holy Spirit, and an unseen and awe-inspiring power works through them, They are the Word personified, or in the Biblical phrase, 'the Word made flesh which dwells among us.' The Word, or love and power of God in action, is their essence, their inner being, of which they are at all times fully conscious.

The spiritual power of the Holy Spirit of the Supreme Father needs an outlet, a focus through which it can pass to the mind and soul of man if he is to be awakened to spiritual truth. The Spirit is everywhere present, but it must be concentrated through a special outlet to be effective on the earthplane. Electricity exists, but until it is converted and concentrated through a generator it will not flow through the wires and become effective light and power.

It is the same with the Word or Holy Spirit; it must use a channel or wire through which to flow and reveal itself to those who want its light. If it is to help human beings to start the upward journey to their eternal home, it must find an outlet through another human being. Accordingly, God uses his special sons, the Masters, as the channels through which His power can flow to the seekers among mankind.

As Jesus said: 'It is not I, but my Father which is in heaven which doeth these things.'

But still he had to be here on earth in his human form. There had to be an outlet, a human channel through which the Father could speak and act and pour His power.

The Master is not the body. He is the divine power that functions through his body. This boundless power, the Indian scriptures say, 'works without hands, sees without eyes, walks without feet, and hears without ears.' It is the unseen power of God, and to get in touch with it one must approach a perfect Master.

To obtain knowledge of God we must necessarily go to
one who knows God's science and is himself proficient in it.
It is only the person who has a conscious experience or
realisation of God who can impart God-knowledge. Within
the Master there is the one great power of God, and through
him human beings can reach that power. Inwardly, the Master
is at one with the universal spirit, and is entrusted with the
mission of bringing individuals into direct contact with God.

'These eyes of His see through eternity and beyond,'
wrote the Saint, Soami Ji.

'The Master's body is in this material world, but in higher
realms is his soul,' says Shams-i-Tabriz.

And Maulana Rum, explaining the same truth, says:

'With one tongue the Master talks to beings in the higher
spheres, and with the other speaks to mortals like us.'

Every word uttered by a true Master is an expression of
unalterable truth, brought down from higher worlds.

In the Master resides the great power of God, and through
the Masters human beings can reach and contact that power.
The omnipotent power lives in the Master's body, using it as
a vehicle for its manifestations, and thus becomes accessible
to mankind.

Radha Soami disciples—and there are many of them—who
have advanced some distance on the path and have many
times gone with the Master into the higher, heavenly worlds,
have expressed how these spiritual journeys reveal the Masters'
dual nature. The following description of this experience is
adapted from the book *With a Great Master in India:*

Looking at the Master as a mere man, such disciples say,
one can form no conception of his true greatness. But when
one travels with him on the path that passes upward through
the heavenly regions, then, and only then, does one see him
as he really is. There, they say, it is no uncommon sight to
witness hundreds of thousands of souls, all radiant in their

own light, but all following him and worshipping him in loving adoration.

Disciples who have made these journeys add that the throngs that attend the Master in the heavenly realms run even into millions of souls. And the higher up one goes with him, the greater he is seen to be. He is literally and truly the king of kings in all the regions of light and pure spirituality. But returning to earth again, he says never a word about these frequent journeys, and appears among his disciples simply as a loving, patient father ministering to his little children.

It is from dwelling so continually in the higher worlds that the Masters have the highest spiritual knowledge and are able to transmit it. They teach what they have learnt, not on hearsay or from book learning, but through first-hand personal experience. As Jesus said:

> 'Verily, verily, I say unto thee, we speak that we do know, and testify that we have seen.'
>
> *John 3 : 11*

Kabir Sahib pointed out the same truth when, talking to a Pandit well-versed in religious learning, he said:

> 'O Pandit, you and I cannot possibly agree in our conclusions, for you speak of things you have read in sacred texts, while I speak from actual positive experience of my own.'

And Guru Nanak said:

> 'O man, listen to the sublime teachings of the Saints. They give out what they have seen with their own eyes.'

The supreme importance of the Master is made very clear by Dr Julian P. Johnson in his book *With a Great Master in India*. He says:

'This great truth grows upon one as he advances in the study. He finds more and more that the Master is the very centre and substance of the system. Without him there is nothing. And this means that he must be a living Master-not one of past ages.

'No soul can ever be saved from the clutches of Maya (the illusion of this world that conceals the divine reality from our sight) and the Wheel of birth and death (reincarnation in life after life), without the aid of a living Master. There is no other way and there never has been any other way for a single soul to escape. Without the personal intervention and help of a living Master, no one, now or in any past age, has ever been able to shake off the bonds of mind and matter and rise to higher realms. We are all utterly dependent upon his grace for our liberation.'

The Master Sawan Singh Ji also speaks many times of the absolute need for a living Master. Thus he says:

'It is only man that has been endowed by the Almighty with faculties by the development of which he can attain to the highest, provided he is initiated by a perfect Master and works hard to elevate his soul to the higher regions. Without a perfect Master, however hard one may try, he cannot make such progress in the spiritual world.'

The Word, the living vibrant force of the Sound Current, is within man, but the key is with the Master. So long as he does not apply the key, the Word and the Way remain behind fast-closed doors. But once the Master has given his initiation and has opened the disciple's inner ears, the enchanting and other-worldly strains of the divine music may be heard and the disciple can start on his journey to the heaven worlds. For the Sound Current is literally the Way by which we ascend and return to our eternal home.

No soul can ever escape from this dark material world without conscious participation in and a personal relationship with this current of God's Power. One must merge himself in that life stream and soaring aloft upon it, or borne upward by it, he will rise to spiritual liberation or salvation. The

upward journey cannot be made in any other way. It is
through their gift of the life stream and their inner
identification with it that the Masters are the Way. And
without the Master's aid, we cannot find the Way. This is the
manner in which Jesus and other spiritual Masters are the
Way, and are able to put our feet on the upward path. There
is no other method of making our homeward journey.

Thus, it is possible to enter upon the Way only with the aid
of a living Master; and the Master is also needed as a guide
as the soul rises higher and higher into the realms of light. No
one can make this radiant journey—the supreme adventure of
the soul—alone and unaided.

On this point the *Adi Granth* says:

> 'Remember, none findeth God without the Master's help;
> millions of efforts will be of no avail without meeting the
> Guru.'

And Maulana Rum points the way by saying:

> 'Whoever wishes to sit near the Lord, tell him to sit at the
> feet of the Master.'

There have always been perfect spiritual Masters on the
earth; the fact that many of them have lived in India helps to
explain why India has so often been called the 'cradle of
religion.' Many of the people of India are by nature more
sensitive than those of the west, their minds are less sceptical
and restless, and they are more habitually turned towards
religious devotion. In the west, people make untold sacrifices
to obtain business or financial success. But in India and other
eastern countries thousands put forth untold effort to win the
secrets of the science of the soul. In this field of endeavour,
India has always led the world, for throughout recorded
history she has made spiritual exploration her chief
preoccupation and knowing, where others guessed, has charted

the way. And to many of today, it seems that eastern spirituality is to come again, to deliver the western world from its materialism.

An analysis that points out very clearly some of the major contrasts between the east and west is given by L. Adams Beck in *The Story of Oriental Philosophy*. She says:

'The East. . . spiritual and other-wordly, leisured, tolerant of all faiths and philosophies, moving on vast spiritual orbits about the central sun. The West eager, hurried, wordly, absorbed in practical and temporary affairs, opinionated, contemptuous of other peoples and faiths, money-loving less for money's sake than its pursuit, younger, infinitely younger in taste and psychic development than the East.

'In India the soul was free from the beginning to choose what it would, each path shadowing forth some different aspect of the One whom in the inmost chambers of her heart India has always adored. Therefore the spiritual outlook was universal. Each took unrebuked what he needed. The children were at home in the house of the Father, while Europe crouched under the lash of a capricious Deity whose ways were beyond all understanding.'

And so, in the east, today as for thousands of years past, it is well known that it is the living Master, and the living Master alone, who can show the seeker the Way and bring him to the Supreme Father. For there is a well-marked way known to the Masters that leads us out of the troubles of this world and into the blessed realms of peace and light. It is a spiritual Way, and also a scientific one. By one great Indian Master, it has been called 'the science of connecting the individual soul with its Creator.' It can bring to its followers not only peace of mind and soul, but above all, it can give them direct knowledge of God and make them one with God. And this, little though it may be realised today, is the ultimate destiny of all who are genuine spiritual seekers.

In concluding this chapter, it may be pointed out that no true Master ever accepts money for this help and teaching. He lives on his own income, whatever it may be, and in no way depends on the support of others. The rich and the poor, the high and the low, all recieve the same loving attention from the Master, without any thought of fees or payments. This, therefore, is a simple test of a perfect Master. If you meet anyone who claims to be a Master, but charges for his spiritual instructions, you may know at once that he is not a genuine Master, who can connect you with the Word and lead you back to your spiritual home. In this connection, Guru Nanak says:

> 'Touch not the feet of those who call themselves Gurus or Pirs and who go a-begging. Only he who works for his bread and out of his earning spares something for charity knows the Path.'

As nature offers mankind light, water, air, and other blessings freely to one and all, so do the Masters offer the doctrine of Him who sent them into the world, the gift of realised spirituality, the positive promise of salvation.

CHAPTER 8

THAT YE MIGHT BE SAVED

'These things I say, that ye might be saved.'
— *John 5 : 34*

The word 'religion' comes from the Latin verb *religare*, meaning to 'bind back', that is, to bind back or reunite the soul with its Creator. It has somewhat the same meaning as the Indian word 'yoga', which means union—union with God.

When Jesus told those whom he accepted as disciples that they would be saved, he meant that he would show them how to find the Way back to union with God. He would give them the keys to the kingdom, and would put their feet on the path that would lead them to the abode of the Father, who loves them with an infinite Love and waits for their return.

And this is the true purpose of all *real* religions—to enable struggling and suffering human beings to find their way back to actual union with their Creator.

'Religion means union of the individual soul with its source', says the Master Sawan Singh Ji. He adds: 'In actual practice, religion is rising up by following the Sound Current'.

Why has man throughout all time possessed an unextinguishable spiritual yearning, arising from deep within him? Because the true man, the inner self or soul, is one with God and longs to return to Him. For man, if he but knew himself, is now and always has been a spiritual being, bright and radiant from God.

In this human life on earth, the great tragedy is that the vast majority of men have lost all knowledge of this fact, and do not know or care to know of the shining path that can lead them back to their Father and their true home.

Religion, the churches tell us, has as its ultimate aim the redemption and salvation of mankind. And this—the salvation of individual human beings—was what Jesus offered to those who listened to his words. It is, moreover, the gift that is offered to all who wish to receive it by the living Masters of today.

Precisely what salvation may mean is, as so often happens in theological matters, not always very clearly understood. This is partly due to the fact that the English word 'salvation', derived from the Latin, does not convey the meaning of the original Greek word used by the writers of the Gospels. This word was much closer to the meaning of the term employed by Jesus.

The Greek word—*soteria*—means simply 'a safe return'. That is all. Our prodigal wanderings in the lower worlds at last completed and our lessons learnt, the time has now come for a safe return to the realm of the Father from which we descended long ago.

The mission of the Masters is to awaken men to the spiritual life and to bring salvation to mankind, to give them here and now the 'safe return' to their true home where they will be reunited with their heavenly Father and Creator.

The Masters come to this earth to give liberty to captive souls, to awaken and revivify souls that have lost touch with God due to long association with mind and matter, and to deliver them from bondage to this world. They reawaken the bond of love between the soul and its Creator and pave the way for reunion. They themselves have attained salvation, and their teaching and guidance can and do lead others to salvation. This they do by bringing souls into touch with the spiritual power of the Word, the Holy Spirit.

Throughout the ages, all of the great Masters have emphasised their role as the saviours of those who were ready and willing to follow them.

Jesus made several statements regarding this part of his earthly mission:

'These things I say that ye might be saved.'

John 5 : 34

'I am the door; by me if any man enter in, he shall be saved.'

John 10 : 9

'For the son of Man is come to seek and to save that which was lost.'

Luke 19 : 10

'For God sent not his Son into the world to condemn the world; but that the world through him might be saved.'

John 3 : 17

The *Adi Granth* contains many references to the function of the Masters as the saviours of mankind:

'Beyond birth and death is he (the Master), and for our good doth he come into the world. Life he giveth us, and devotion he inspireth in us, and with the Lord doth he unite us.'

'Without Sat Guru no one ever found God; without Sat Guru no one ever findeth Him.'

'The Guru is the mediator, He takes man to God.

'Guru is the ship, and Guru is the Captain of the ship. Without Guru no one crosseth the ocean of the world. By Guru's grace do we find the Lord; without Guru is no salvation.

'God himself enshrines His Power in the Master, and that mouthpiece of God has the power to rescue millions.

'With just an atom or a grain of his Power, he (the Master) can save millions of souls.'

According to Hafiz:

'If seekest thou union with God, O thou religious man, then come under the shelter of the Master, the Lord of both the worlds, and crave thou his help. Then indeed shalt thou live in peace.'

Guru Nanak says:

'If by ourselves could we find union with God, why should we have suffered the pangs of separation? Nay, only through the Masters do we realise Him, O Nanak, and experience true rapture.'

Sri Ramakrishna emphasises:

'When a perfect Master comes (to this earth), innumerable are the men who find Salvation by taking refuge in Him.'

And the great Master Sawan Singh Ji writes:

'The sole mission and sole interest of the saints is to make people go in and, with the help of the True Word, reach their original Spiritual Home whence they came. The principles of Sant Mat are eternal and immutable, and all saints from times immemorial, whether in this or any other land, have preached the same doctrine of the Word as the only means of true salvation.'

The living Master is the very centre and soul and substance of the Way of salvation laid down by the Supreme Father. Without the love and help of a living Master, no soul can ever be liberated from the material world and return to its eternal home. It is the Master alone who is commissioned by God to show us the Way back, and to guide us on the path.

To receive the help of the Master, it is necessary for an individual to realise his own helplessness, his utter inability to rise to the higher regions without the Master's continual and powerful spiritual aid. This is such an important factor and such a new concept to many, that it requires great emphasis.

'The masses of mankind are hopelessly entangled in the meshes of mind and matter', says Dr Julian P. Johnson in his foreword to the Sar Bachan. 'The individual cannot disentangle himself and effect his escape. He can only struggle, and the struggle generally leaves him worse off than he was before. No method of religious ceremony, study, ritual, pilgrimage or prayers can extricate him. Not even good works of charity can save him. Moreover, he should remember that even God Himself cannot save him, if he depends upon God to do it by direct intervention. God has a very definite method of accomplishing His work. The divine and natural method admits of no substitute. This helpless and destitute condition of the individual soul is the very first lesson to be learnt.

'This then leads us to the second great truth, which is a natural corollary of the first, viz. the vital necessity for a living Master.

'To acquire salvation, to accomplish liberation from the wheel (of births and deaths) . . . every soul must find a Guru, or Master. This is the divine method. The work (of salvation) can be accomplished in no other way. The Master is the Lord of life and death. He is able to save; and without Him there is no escape.'

Again, it must be emphasised here that the path that leads to salvation must be entered upon during one's lifetime, not after one's death. The contact with the Master and the Sound Current must be made while one is living on this earth.

'During thy lifetime do thou seek realisation (of God), O brother,' says the great Saint, Kabir Sahib. 'For while living doth a man understand, knoweth he while living, and

while living doth he attain salvation. If here dost thou find
Him, then shalt thou meet Him hereafter.'

The Master Sawan Singh Ji is even more outspoken. He
says:

> 'Reliance on salvation after death is the finest form of self-
> deception man practises on himself. If there is no salvation
> during life, it will not come after death. He who is illiterate
> when alive cannot be a scholar after death.'

And the same truth was underscored by the Apostle Paul
when he wrote to the Corinthians:

'Behold, now is the accepted time; behold, now is the day
of salvation.'

It is not intended that we should merely resign ourselves
and hope for salvation after death. The safe return can be
made, and according to the divine plan of the Creator, must
be made while one is still alive. This is done by following the
age-old path of the Masters. Of this, the masters, including
Master Jesus, have assured mankind over and over again. To
each and every one of their disciples they say:

'Come, let us return to our own home. Why live in a
foreign land?'

When, with the Master's aid, the disciple begins to hear
the celestial music of the Sound Current, a new and higher
longing begins to fill his heart and mind. He becomes
dissatisfied with his old way of life and begins to aspire to
something higher and finer. His love for the Master and the
Supreme Father who works through the Master increases and
soon becomes the most important factor in his life. There is
no other experience on earth that can possibly mean so much
as the joy of being in his serene and gracious presence,
sharing in his love and absorbing his spiritual light; feeling
within oneself his gentle but irresistible God-Power ever at
work cleansing and purifying the mind and soul, re-creating

one in the form of his own divine image. There is no joy to equal that of knowing through direct experience that the beloved Master is leading one step by step up the path of the safe return—the path that leads at last to the eternal home, whose beauties, joy, and bliss are indescribable in earthly language and beyond the comprehension of the human mind.

CHAPTER 9

A FAR COUNTRY

'And not many days after, the younger son gathered all together, and took his journey into a far country, and there wasted his substance with riotous living.

Luke 15 : 13

In the parable of the prodigal son, Jesus epitomised the story of all humanity. This is the story of the descent of the soul from its original home in Sat Desh, the real country, of its wandering for many ages in the lower worlds, and of its eventual return to its Father's house.

All other great Masters have told the same story in various ways. It is a story that they must tell in carrying out their work of teaching men that they are spiritual beings who are now living in a very imperfect world, far lower than that from which they originally came.

In the east, the leading figure of the story—the soul—is often compared to a beautiful and rich princess who wanders away from her palace. Finding herself in new and unfamiliar surroundings, her mind becomes clouded and in the end she lays aside her royal robes, clothes herself in rags, and becomes a companion of sweepers and servants (the mind and the senses).

It may be noted here that the story of Adam and Eve is but another version of this same allegory. The much-misinterpreted 'fall of man' and the consequent 'original sin', upon which certain churches have built up an entire system of man-made theology, is simply another version of the story of the descent of the soul from its true home to the 'far country' of the material world.

The Descent of the Soul

Originally, as has been pointed out, all individuals who have lived or now live on this earth dwelt as spiritual beings, or souls, in Sat Desh, the region of pure Spirit.

Hafiz, the Persian Master, expressed this truth when he exclaimed:

'O Hafiz, the highest spiritual heaven is our ancestral Home.'

This was our native place, in which, countless ages ago, the Supreme Father brought us into being as individual and immortal souls, each soul being of the very essence of the Father. As one of the Indian Upanishads says:

'This is the truth: As from a blazing fire in a thousand ways sparks proceed, so, O beloved, are produced living souls from the indestructible Creator, and to Him they return.'

Each soul is a spark of the divine flame, and the relationship between the Supreme Creator and the soul was, and still is a relationship of intense love.

For aeons we dwelt in our true home. But on separation from the Father the souls obtained their own individuality, which bore within it potential egotism; and also limited free will—the God-given gift of choice to take the upward or the downward path. And in the end, countless souls ventured forth like the prodigal son and set out to explore the beauties and delights of the regions below Sat Desh. Gradually, over a long period of time, these souls descended through the different spheres, and many of them came at last to the physical universe. We who are now on earth are some of these souls. We, in fact, are the prodigal sons.

How long ago the descent of the soul took place, history does not record, for the life span of the historical civilisations known to us is very brief, a matter of some five or six thousand years. But the Masters, whose knowledge of human history on this earth extends over a far longer period, say that many individuals who are now on earth have been coming here in different forms for many millions of years.

We came down through the higher worlds and finally came into this world. But once here, we became absorbed in the fascinating panorama of the show and lost all recollection of our Father. The Masters sometimes compare us with a child who goes to a fair holding onto his father's hand, but lets go of the father's hand and wanders happily on looking at the many attractions of the fair, even hoping that his father will not find him to take him home.

During the course of its descent, the soul stayed for some time in the region of universal mind, and here it came under the sway of the region's ruler, Kal, whom the Masters call the negative power. At the same time, each individual soul became associated with an individual mind, derived from universal mind. This individual mind is of the essence of Kal, and serves, even today, as the agent of Kal as we go about our daily affairs here on earth. It operates to keep us confined to the material world by developing worldly desires and attachments, to shut us off from the music of the Sound Current, to make us forgetful of our Father, and to obliterate all memories of our divine origin and our true home in Sat Desh. For one of Kal's duties is to keep us imprisoned in the material world until, purified and made wiser by manifold experiences, we begin to search for the path that can lead us to the far finer life of the higher regions.

While in the realm of universal mind, the soul also put on the covering of the causal or mental body, which it needed in order to function in this so-called causal or mental world and communicate with others who dwell there.

The mind is made of a very fine and subtle form of matter, and is in very close communion with the soul. It can be thought of as a fine sheath or garment covering the soul.

The causal or mental body is also composed of very fine matter. It may be regarded as a portion of the mind itself, but constituting a second covering around the soul. This body is man's highest and finest instrument of action, except mind itself. It is through this body that the soul contacts all of the lower levels of life, working through the astral and physical bodies.

When the soul became associated with mind, which has outward and downward tendencies quite opposite to the soul's own inward and upward-looking nature, the so-called 'fall of man' entered its first phase. For it was at this time that the soul first became subject to the influences of mind and matter, both the mind and the causal body being made of matter, though of a high order of fitness.

The association with mind and matter, which enormously hampers the soul in expressing itself, is symbolised by the marriage of Adam, the divine and immortal soul of man, to Eve, who stands as a symbol of matter. After this marriage the individual entity was no longer pure spirit, as it was in the brighter, higher realms of its home. The marriage, in effect, made it dual in nature and caused it to enter upon the first stages of indulgence in sense pleasures. For it was only after the soul was wedded to the mind and causal body that the individual was for the first time capable of harmful self-indulgence. It was then that mind and matter really commenced to cloud the inner spirituality of the soul.

From the region of universal mind the soul, wrapped in its new coverings, continued its downward journey and descended to the next region below—the astral plane. Here it was necessary for it to assume the astral body in order to be able to function and communicate with others.

This body reflects in its form and colours the true character of the individual. Everyone who can see it can know at once the purity or other qualities of its possessor. On the astral plane everyone is seen exactly as he is, and no deception is possible. The astral body has its five senses, just as does the physical body.

Remaining for some time in the astral region, the soul next descended to the material world, and here it needed a physical body. With the addition of this body the soul was wrapped in four coverings—the physical body, astral body, causal body and mind. And with each covering that it put on its light was dimmed, and it was still further shut off from the life-giving Word or power of its Creator. At the same time, the soul in this world is associated with the pleasure-loving mind, and must contact the material world through the mind and the five senses. Otherwise, it could not perceive and receive impressions of the material objects and people that surround it here.

Under these conditions the soul, far away from its original home, lonely and lost, is subject to all the worldly and downward pulling desires of the mind, the senses, and the five evil passions—lust, anger, greed, attachment and ego. Inevitable conflict is the result, for there is a never-ending struggle in every human being between the immortal longings of the soul and the material desires of the mind.

This is the spiritual plight of all mankind today, the Supreme Father's prodigal sons who now dwell in this country so far-distant from their homeland.

'Why did the soul lose its supremacy?' asks the Master Sawan Singh. 'Because it lost touch with the Word and associated with the mind.'

How can the soul regain its supermacy? By becoming once more connected with the divine Word. And this, as has been pointed out, is the special work for which the Supreme Father sends His Saints and Masters down into the darkness of the material worlds. To those who sincerely long for deliverance, the living Master will reveal the shining path that leads back from this far country in which we now dwell to our homeland in the highest heavenly regions.

In all ages the Masters have been moved with compassion at seeing the pitiable condition of human beings in this world, as compared with their previous existence in the radiantly pure and blissful regions of Sat Desh. And in all ages they have done all that they could to urge the wanderers in this dark world to start the journey back to their true home.

Maulana Rum of Persia told those who would listen to him:

'Recollect thou that which is from the blissful Spiritual Realms, but which now cometh not into thy memory. Since those realms thou hast forgotten, hence art thou helpless and bewildered.'

And Shams-i-Tabriz, another of the great Persian Masters, pleaded with ignorant and wayward mankind, urging them:

'Go thou up into the meadow where first thou wert, for enough hast thou wandered in this wilderness.'

And every other perfect Master has delivered the self-same message, to which most men have impatiently turned a deaf ear. In the end, however, all true spiritual seekers will heed the message, for that is the purpose of the Creator's divine plan. And the love and mercy of the Supreme One are never-failing and never-ending. He is indeed long-suffering and infinitely patient. No matter how long it may take the prodigal sons and daughters to come to their senses and start their homeward journey, always the light will be kept burning in their Father's palace, and the Father will be waiting, ready to welcome the wanderers home.

CHAPTER 10

BORN OF THE FLESH

'That which is born of the flesh is flesh; and that which is born of the Spirit is spirit.'
—*John 3 : 6*

Here, in the material world, where the real self of man, the soul, is imprisoned in a body of flesh, most of mankind is in spiritual darkness, though this fact is seldom recognised. When we are born of the flesh, the soul is out of touch with the life-giving Word and, in most cases, is shut off completely from the higher, happier worlds.

In addition, due to the soul's association with the mind, it has forgotten its divine origin. As a result, men are not aware of their principal and primary duty. This is to turn away from this world and return to the infinitely higher dwelling place of the Supreme Father.

If man but knew his real self, the soul, he would find that in its own sphere of action, and when freed of the mind, it has tremendous power. But here, in the coarse and dense material world, its power is suppressed and, so to speak, smothered under the coverings of the mind and the various bodies.

The Masters say that when the soul is born into a body of flesh, it is like a brightly shining lamp that is covered over with several pieces of heavy cloth—the mind, the causal body, the astral body and the gross physical body. The brilliant radiance of the soul is undimmed, but it cannot penetrate its coverings. These shut it in far more than men realise, and prevent its powers of action and expression from functioning at more than a fraction of their great potential.

Under these conditions, most human beings are virtually dead, spiritually. But they do not know it. They do not know, for example, that above and beyond this world there are innumerable other and much superior worlds, filled with light, beauty and true happiness. They do not realise that even the best life in this world is a drab and dreary affair as compared with the freer, happier and more spiritual life of these higher worlds. They do not know that if one looks down upon this world, as the Masters and many of their disciples do from the higher regions, the earth resembles a dirty slum or tenement district surrounded by clouds of darkness created by the evil thoughts of men. They do not know that it is possible to enter and visit the higher worlds while still living here in the human body and that this is the path that all men must and will follow—in due time.

Relatively speaking, all things of this world are transient and temporary. All human experiences are transitory, and our whole span of life in the flesh is only one of many short episodes in the ages-long history of the spiritually beautiful soul which, like its Creator, is deathless and eternal. We are not here to live forever. Actually, in the divine plan for our redemption, the material world is only a camping ground, where we stay for short periods from time to time during our journey back to our eternal home. As Omar Khayam's *Rubaiyat* says in all truth:

> 'Tis but a Tent where takes his one day's rest
> A Sultan to the realm of Death addresst
> The Sultan rises, and the dark Farrash
> Strikes, and prepares it for another Guest.'

The pleasures of this life are not only short-lived but only too often turn into bitterness or disappointment. In reality,

when one rises up and begins to know the truth, with the
Master's help and guidance, he sees that worldly happiness
is no more than an illusion, a mirage; for what seems to be
happiness is momentary pleasure and only too often brings
sufferings of some kind in its wake. The fact is, as the
Masters teach and universal experience confirms, there is no
lasting peace or happiness in the pleasures of this world.

On this point Guru Nanak says:

> 'All the world is in pain and grief; only he is happy who
> dwells in Nam (the Word).'

And Sehjo Bai, the famous holy woman of Rajasthan says:

> 'All the wealthy I have found unhappy; all the poor are the
> picture of pain.
> 'Sehjo! only lovers of God are in peace, having found the
> secret of the Name.'

Actually, there is only one real pleasure, one genuine
happiness open to human beings, which never ends in
disappointment, painful reactions, remorse or regrets. This is
the joy of listening to the divine melodies of the Sound
Current and of being borne upwards by them towards the
Father's—our Father's—home.

'Brothers', says Guru Nanak, 'only those are truly happy
who reach their eternal home.'

Here, few situations are permanently free of pain; and for
many, as the French writer Albert Camus has said, life on this
earth may best be described as 'the long anguish of living and
dying.' Sooner or later, life deals all of us heavy blows that
sicken or sadden the heart. Sooner or later, we all have our
tears to weep.

Human life and the pleasures of this world are such a
kaleidoscopic affair. Here today, gone tomorrow. In this

ever-changing life happiness co-exists with misery, fortune with misfortune, prosperity with adversity, companionship with separation, health with illness, enjoyment with anxiety; each follows the other like scenes in a play.

And we, too, are like actors in a play. Like actors, we attach the utmost importance to playing our human roles, striving for success, for money or for fame, in whatever role we are cast and becoming so deeply involved in the play that we forget our real life, the life of the spirit. The play of material life becomes all-absorbing, just as a drama seems real to the actors when they identify themselves fully with their parts. But the play of human life is only for the time being—a temporary phase in the far greater drama of the immortal soul.

How many of the actors are genuinely happy? How many, under the polite masks, they show the world, are leading, as Thorean surmised, lives of quiet desparation? And how many are there who, though outwardly serene and poised, are inwardly filled with doubts and uncertainties, emptiness, loneliness or bitterness, regrets for the past and fears for the future? Most thinking persons who have pondered upon the problems of this world have found it in very truth a sorry place. Mankind today, perhaps more than in any other age, seems to have gone astray, to have taken—oftentimes deliberately and rebelliously—the wrong path. The world today seems willing to try every way except the right way.

It has been said that nowadays the world is filled with the results of intellectual and scientific activity—and of spiritual inactivity. Certain it is, in any event, that spiritual darkness broods over the world today and to many millions of human beings, life consists largely of trials, tears and troubles, while to some it is a tragedy.

'For the world which seems
To lie before us like a land of dreams,

So various, so beautiful, so new,
Hath really neither joy, nor love, nor light,
Nor certitude, nor peace, nor help for pain;
And we are here as on a darkling plain
Swept with confused alarms of struggle and flight,
Where ignorant armies clash by night.'

So wrote the English poet Matthew Arnold. And though his indictment of the world may seem harsh, there are only too many whose experiences here bear out his well-considered testimony.

These truths, like some of the others that have been taught throughout the ages by the spiritual Masters, are unfamiliar and in some cases distasteful to many people in the west. For western people have been prone to maintain, against all contradictory evidence, that 'everything is for the best in this best of all possible worlds,' and that 'Gods' in His heaven— all's right with the world.'

This is the philosophy needed by some and, indeed, the philosophy that is officially endorsed by the leading western religious organisations. But thoughtful persons are well aware that in this world there is much that falls short of perfection. And the truth of the matter is, according to the teaching of the Masters, that this world is not intended to be a perfect or even a near-perfect one. It is in one of the lowest parts of the entire Creation, and one of its purposes is to serve, if the truth be known, as a kind of reform school for wayward souls. This world is either a school, a hospital, or a prison. But it is never a paradise. There are relatively few, however, who are willing to accept this fundamental truth, at least when it is first presented to them.

It is not intended to paint too dark a picture of human life. Some joy is to be found here too. But basically this world is a testing ground. The truth is that it is God's kindergarten. The Masters often call it the 'prison house of mind and matter.'

'This world, which is a wilderness, has been mistaken for a residence', says Soami Ji in the *Sar Bachan*. 'It's good things which are all perishable are taken for the true and real, while that which is actually real is altogether lost sight of.'

Here, all are tested in one way or another for the earth is not meant to be a place of unalloyed happiness, as so many suppose. God's purpose is that character should be tested, oftentimes up to the hilt, while we are here on earth.

Mind and Soul

When we are born of the flesh we are, in most cases, born into a life in which the soul is to a large extent dominated by the mind and the mind's inherent love for things of this world. Under these conditions, the soul, which is sometimes called the witness self, can watch everything that takes place, but cannot always control the wayward and wilful impulses of the mind.

Defining the position of the soul, one of the Indian Upanishads says:

'Unseen but seeing, unheard but hearing, unperceived but perceiving, unknown but knowing, this is thy Self, the ruler within, the immortal.'

It should always be remembered that the soul is the real living entity, and a reality of the first order. It is made of the essence of the Supreme One, our true God. The mind, however, is inert, unless activated by the soul, and is a reality of the second order, for it is made of the essence of Kal, the negative power. Kal is powerful, there is no doubt about that; but he can use only the limited powers assigned to him by the Supreme Lord God.

It should also be remembered that the one thing for which we have been born into this world is the liberation of our souls from the bondage of mind and matter. Relatively speaking, nothing else matters or is worth bothering about. Self-improvement, which to a large extent means purifying the mind, is our principal duty, our most sacred obligation. So the Masters repeat, over and over again.

When regarded from the Masters' point of view, life on this earth is largely a struggle between the mind and the soul. For when we are born of the flesh the soul is in the enemies' country. And the enemies are the mind and its good friends, the senses, and the five evil passions—lust, anger, greed, attachment to worldly things and people, and pride, vanity or egotism.

It is the mind, with its ceaseless activity and love for worldly things and people that stands between the soul and God. It is the one great obstacle—until the time comes that it is brought to knees and trained to concentrate on spiritual matters.

'Strictly speaking', says the Master Sawan Singh, 'we are living an abnormal life. Soul combined with mind and matter is an abnormality. Soul, the queen of royal blood, enjoying the company of servants and sweepers (the mind, the senses, and the five evil passions) is an abnormality.'

Under these conditions, the soul functions under handicaps of the utmost severity. Beautiful, pure and spiritually powerful though it may be, it is in most men under the influence of and dominated by the mind. And the mind, as has been said, is the soul's most dangerous and determined enemy.

The chief function of the mind is to serve as an instrument of the soul for all contacts with the material world. It is an extremely useful instrument, provided it is kept under control. It can be an excellent servant; but if it gets the upper hand it is a bad and vicious master. In the mass of mankind, the mind is the master and willingly follows the promptings of the senses.

The mind, it should be thoroughly understood, has a close

fellowship with the senses and enjoys expressing itself through the five evil passions. These worldly passions or desires, with which all men are familiar, have been described as wild beasts roaming the world, seeking whom they may devour. They are the chief instruments used by the negative power and its agent here on earth, the mind, its offspring, to bind us to the material world. They seek always to draw us to objects of sense and what the Masters call 'the filth of sensual pleasures'. And sensuality, the Masters teach, is death, while spirituality is life.

Thus, in many if not most individuals, the senses and one or another of the five passions overwhelm the mind, and the mind in turn enslaves the soul. It often happens that the soul is quite unable to control its own mental instrument. If that instrument, bound on following the five evil passions, becomes too unruly and rebellious, the soul is powerless.

The Masters sometimes say that the mind is like a rogue elephant. It goes about unrestrained wherever it likes and drags the soul along with it.

At other times the Masters compare the mind dominated by the five passions to a camel without a guiding string. It is likely at any moment to stampede and run away, and it may then run madly on to its own destruction. Under such conditions the soul is helpless. It can only sit back and suffer in silence while the mind revels in its own debasement.

Subtle and powerful in its own right, the mind, working hand in glove with the senses, imprisons the soul and prevents it from returning to the spiritual regions which are its native habitat. Constantly occupied with thoughts and desires connected with the people, pleasures, and activities of the material world, it acts as a heavy veil between the soul and the heavenly melodies of the Word.

It is for these reasons that the Indian sages have always

taught that 'the mind is the veil', and 'the mind is the slayer of the real.'

Soami Ji of Agra points out in the *Sar Bachan:*

> 'Soul is surrounded by enemies (in this world). Even the mind watches it just as a cat does a mouse which it intends to devour.'

The struggle between the soul and the mind and passions explains the enigmatic nature of man. He is a paradoxical creature, capable of rising to the sublimest heights of nobility and spiritual aspiration, and yet equally capable of sinking to the lowest depth.

The mind, dominated by desire and attachments to the world and its transitory pleasures, is the cause of our bondage. The soul, ever yearning, albeit silently, to return to its own home, attains liberation through the practice of Nam—bhakti.

Wrapped up in the never-ceasing activity of the mind, the average person looks at the show of life and forgets that he possesses a soul or, to put it more accurately, that he is a soul. Says Guru Arjun Dev, the fifth Sikh Master:

'When the mind is smitten by countless desires, and is overshadowed all the time by avarice, there is no place therein left for God.'

It is because the mind clings to the material world with such an almost fanatical tendency that we who are born of the flesh are so deeply steeped in materialism. And the deadly enemy of man's spiritual progress is this same materialism, which nourishes in man desire for the material world.

That the mind is so great an enemy of the soul is a new idea to many people in the west. It seems incredible, since it upsets their life-long ideas. Yet the fact remains that it is part of the divine plan of the Supreme Creator. This plan calls for the evolution of man through the material and mental worlds, and the ultimate victory of the soul over the forces of mind and matter.

It is not intended, the Masters say, that we regain our divinity automatically, without any effort of our own. We are meant to strengthen ourselves by struggling for the light, and struggle we must. And the beginning of the struggle is the effort to subjugate the mind and make it the willing servant of the true self.

It may be pointed out here that the mind can never be controlled by negation or efforts to suppress its strong desires. That simply cannot be done. Negation has only a temporary effect. The fire is only covered with ashes, and will flare up again when the winds of passion blow. The materialism of the mind cannot be overcome by using its own material-mental weapons, nor can the mind be conquered on its own ground. Like Antaeus, it thrives and grows ever stronger so long as it can keep its feet upon the earth. But when it is lifted above the earth by a higher power, it weakens and finally succumbs.

To permanently control the mind, it must be given something that it enjoys better than the worldly pleasures, and the only thing that can supply this need is the divine music and spiritual power of the Sound Current. As a consequence, any method of spiritual development that does not make the Sound Current the vital factor in its system of spiritual exercises can never counteract the downward drag of the mind and senses. But once the mind has experienced the joy of listening to the divine melody, it will become attached to it for good and its interest in the soul-destroying sense pleasures will come to an end. The Word of God, or the Sound Current, is the one and only successful means of permanent mind control by which a struggling human being, sore beset, can overcome the mind's good friends, the five evil passions, and liberate himself from all worldly desires and downward tendencies.

The mind is a power that can bind us to earth, and it can also set us free, depending on how it is used. Most people unconsciously, and even wilfully, use it for the former purpose. But those who follow the path of the Masters consciously use it to regain their lost freedom. We have attached ourselves to this world by thinking always of worldly things. But we can escape from the material world in the same way, that is, by meditating on God and the higher worlds in the manner taught by the perfect Masters, and thereby becoming attached to the divine Sound Current.

Divine qualities constitute the essence of our true self. Purity, peace and bliss are the eternal characteristics of our inner being. And as a result, man's inner hunger for spiritual unfoldment cannot forever be satisfied by the pleasures of this earth life. Unceasingly, through days and years of alternating joy and sorrow, quietude and storms, the eternal longing of the soul calling from within the temple, is ever trying to make itself known to the outer man. But many ignore its divine promptings or refuse to heed its gentle pleading.

Confined within the body and duped and dominated by the mind, man is limited. But in his soul he is limitless. Hidden within him is a priceless jewel, though he knows it not.

'None is poor, O Bhikha', says Bhikha Sahib. 'Every one hath rubies in his bundle. But how to untie the knot he doth not know, and therefore he is a pauper.'

Throughout the world today many have forgotten the existence of their sublime and peaceful inner self, and their lives are troubled. But the self, in its long and patient vigil, has never forgotten us.

'God is in all men', says Shri Ramakrishna, 'but all men are not in God. That is why they suffer.'

The first step towards freeing the soul from its captivity is mastery of the pleasure-loving mind.

Says Guru Nanak:

'Conquer the mind, and you conquer the world.'

And Maulana Rum, fully aware of the spiritual plight of mankind and pointing the way to the higher, better life, exclaims:

'Whoever curbeth the flesh, the sun and the clouds doth he command.'

The control and purification of the mind, accomplished with the aid of a living Master and the Sound Current, leads to the freedom of the soul and awareness of the spiritual realms.

'Spiritual progress primarily depends on the training of the mind', says Master Sawan Singh Ji, in speaking of this particular aspect of the path. 'In ordinary man the soul is under the control of the mind, and the mind is controlled by the senses, and the senses are led away by the objects of senses. The attention thus remains wandering from object to object (in the material world).

'The right way should be that the senses do not run after the objects, the mind is not led astray by the senses, and the soul has the grip on the mind and uses it as its tool to serve its purpose. The soul is to establish its supremacy over the mind instead of remaining its slave.

'Why did the soul lose its supremacy? Because it lost touch with the Word and associated with the mind. Therefore, there is only one effective method (of enabling the soul to regain its supremacy), and that is bringing the soul in touch with the Word again.'

How to do this in the simplest and most effective way is taught by the perfect Masters and this, as has been pointed out, is the way that the Supreme Father has expressly provided for all who choose to avail themselves of it.

CHAPTER 11

THE KINGDOM IS WITHIN

'The kingdom of God is within you.'
—Luke 17 : 21

'Ye are the temple of the living God.'
—II Corinthians 6 : 16

One of the fundamental truths emphasised by Jesus is the immanence of the kingdom of God, the fact that it is *within* each and every human being. This is also one of the cardinal precepts in the teachings of all other great Masters, including those who are here on this earth today.

They, like Jesus, say that the kingdom of heaven is by no means a far-off place or a state of consciousness to be realised only after death. They teach, and also prove to their disciples, that the kingdom is a very present reality, which can be entered and known in this very life. The present day disciples, as those of the past, are taught how to look within themselves and thereby find the kingdom here and now.

The statement that we must go within is, and always has been, confusing to many. Actually, it means that the higher worlds are reached by withdrawing the attention from the outer world and concentrating it within oneself.

This is done by centring the attention at the third eye, commonly called the eye centre, which is situated between the two eyebrows. When one succeeds in concentrating all of his attention at that point, the attention is actually and literally all inside of him. The outer world has been completely shut out and temporarily forgotten. The whole of the disciple's mind and soul have left the outer world and have 'gone within'.

Every man possesses the third eye, which is a private door that opens on the eternal brightness. As the disciple holds his attention steadily fixed on it, the soul and mind gradually concentrate all their forces there. When this concentration has been successfully achieved, the mind and soul pass through an inner aperture in the forehead called the 'Tenth Door', leave the body, and rise to a higher region.

When the soul in this manner passes through the inner 'gates of light', it enters one of the countless kingdoms of heaven, or mansions of the Father's house. Which one it enters depends upon the degree of spiritual advancement that has been achieved. The kingdom is then spoken of as an 'inner world', and is so called because one must first go within in order to reach it.

Thus, while the physical body is the prison chamber of the soul, it is at the same time the temple of the living God. And it is in this temple that man is intended really to worship God. This truth has also been taught by all of the many great Masters who have visited this earth.

In the *Adi Granth* it is written:

> 'The temple of God is the body, from which come out the rubies of knowledge.'

and:

> 'By the grace of the Master do thou behold, within thyself is the temple of God.'

Maghrabi, a Mohammedan saint, says:

> 'The Beloved resides within you, O ignorant man, and you are searching for Him outside from place to place. If the Beloved be within us, and we go elsewhere to find Him, all our efforts will be in vain. The ignorant bow to the temples, the true seekers always enter the living temples—their bodies.'

The human body is a much more remarkable mechanism than is generally realised. We are in very truth 'fearfully and wonderfully made'. But there are few who know the marvellous manner in which the temple of the human body is constructed.

'Men travel to gaze upon mountain heights and the waves of the sea, broad-flowing rivers and the expanse of the ocean, and pass by themselves, the crowning wonder,' wrote St. Augustine in his *Confessions*.

In brief, the human body is a microcosm, or small universe, a reproduction or epitome of the macrocosm, which is the vast universe of universes.

Man is the microcosm and the universe is the macrocosm, and the two are very intimately inter-related. Within each human body there are certain parts, or centres, which correspond with allied portions or regions of the higher spiritual worlds. And every part of man, of his physical, his astral, and his causal bodies, has a definite relationship with some particular part of the outer universe and the higher worlds. These inner centres in man can serve as means of communication with their corresponding regions in the outer worlds of space and the heavenly regions.

It is due to this fact that man, when properly instructed and trained by a perfect Master, is able to leave his body and achieve conscious communication with any or all parts of the universe—those vast, beautiful and happy regions inhabited by numberless hosts of beings who are like ourselves, or are superior to us.

'Whatever is in the universe is also in the body,' says the Master Pipa Sahib. 'Whosoever seeketh in the body verily doth he find.'

And the Master Sawan Singh Ji points out:

'Man is a wonderful creation. He not only carries his past

history with him, but the whole creation—visible and invisible—and the Creator of all are within him, and he has been gifted with capacity to see all that lies in him and to be one with his Creator.'

Everyone knows that the physical brain is in touch with all parts of the body through the nervous system. In a corresponding manner, there are in the astral body certain centres by means of which man can get in touch with the entire astral world. In like manner other centres serve as points of departure for communication with their corresponding higher and finer worlds. This contact is established, and the various centres are awakened, by means of concentrated attention at the point, or centre, chosen under the direction of the Master. By concentrated attention at any given centre, the consciousness is awakened at that centre, and from there the awakened consciousness moves upward towards those subtler and more beautiful worlds which are correlated to that centre.

St. Augustine, who had gone within the body and so to the worlds beyond, expressed this truth in the words:

'I came with the flesh, through flesh, to Him who is beyond the flesh.'

We are not confined to this physical body, even while we are still living in it. We are imprisoned in the body only because we do not know how to get out of it.

The soul is enclosed in the confines of the flesh and until we learn how to take our soul out of this confinement, we cannot see the higher worlds, nor have true knowledge or real bliss. It is the perfect Master alone who can teach us how to do this. As Maulana Rum says in his inimitable style:

'Save Saints and Masters, who else can liberate mankind from the confinement of this magical box (the body)?'

The Masters teach us how to gain our freedom, and the journey that liberates us commences within the temple of the human body. When with the help and guidance of the Master, the threshold of the temple is passed, the soul finds itself in the heavenly kingdoms. Then it finds transcendental knowledge, cosmic consciousness, the divine light, and the living God.

At the time of initiation the Master gives the new disciple exact instructions as to how to proceed to enter the first of the heavenly kingdoms. This is the astral plane. It is in this region and the lower portion of the region next above—the second stage on the upward path of the Masters—that all the heavens and paradises of the world's organized religions are located.

The method of concentration and meditation taught by the true Masters is the knocking at the door mentioned by Jesus when he said:

> 'Knock, and it shall be opened unto you.'
> *Matthew 7 : 7*

When rightly practised under the guidance of the Master, this method never fails to open the 'tenth door'.

As the student begins to succeed in achieving concentration and going within, one of his first new experiences is to hear the melody of the Sound Current within him. In this connection Kabir Sahib says:

> 'Close thou thine eyes, thine ears, and thy mouth and listen to the subtle Eternal Music.'

And Maulana Rum, urging the disciple to practise the form of meditation taught by the perfect Masters, says:

> 'O, close thou thine eyes, thine ears, and thy lips; and if the secret of God thou dost not behold, then laugh thou at me.'

It is by concentrating within ourselves that we hear the transcendent and all-powerful sound of the Word. Although its music is omnipresent, still we cannot come into contact with it unless we are taught how to look inwards or go within. In this sense the Eternal Voice is within us; it is in the subtle spiritual realms into which we can gain access only by collecting our consciousness within ourselves.

Says the *Adi Granth*:

'Inside ourselves is the true Heavenly Melody.'

At the same time that the student begins to hear the divine sound, he also begins to see the celestial light—the radiant light of God that floods the higher regions with its heavenly radiance.

At first he sees a vast starry sky containing what the ancient Vedic scriptures of India described as the path of the Gods. Later he sees the myriad glowing lights of the so-called sun worlds and the moon worlds. All of these lie between the material world and the pure astral regions.

When the astral world is reached, the disciple sees the spiritual light that is the central part of that region. It is from the rays or vibrations of power issuing from this light that our entire universe is being sustained. Out of this light there issues a heavenly sound.

Says the *Adi Granth*:

'Inside us is the Flame, and in that Flame is the Inner Sound that inspireth in us love for the true Lord.'

And in the words of the Master, Paltu Sahib:

'A Voice cometh out of the flame of the Lamp, but he alone who is in the trance of transcendent knowledge heareth it, and none else doth hear.'

It is this experience that Jesus referred to when he said:

> 'If therefore thine eye be single, thy whole body shall be full of light.'
>
> *Matthew 6 : 22*

In other words, when the disciple concentrates his attention at the third eye, the single eye, he will begin to see, with the everpresent help of the Master, the inner or heavenly lights of the spiritual worlds. As he progresses, he sees the much greater and more luminous light of the still higher worlds.

And again, speaking of the experience that comes to every disciple of a living Master who goes within, Jesus said:

> 'I am the light of the world: he that followeth me shall not walk in darkness, but shall have the light of life.'
>
> *John 8 : 12*

Every true Master throughout history has been the light of the world. They have within them the light and spiritual life of the Holy Spirit of the Supreme Father of us all. When a disciple centres his attention on his Master, he walks in his light and sees the brilliant spiritual light within. For him there can then be no more darkness.

This is an elementary truth of the path of the Masters, and even today in this materialistic twentieth century it is known and experienced daily by thousands of disciples. They have opened the gates of light within themselves, guided by the Master's instructions and inner assistance. They have the light of eternal life here and now, because they have faithfully followed their living Master.

Speaking of the light seen by the disciple when he rises to the first heavenly worlds, Guru Nanak says:

> 'Day and night shineth the pure Light, and Guru's devotee knoweth this inner lamp.'

In the same connection the *Adi Granth* says:

'Whosoever by God's grace findeth Sat Guru, in the temple
of his mind is the spiritual lamp lighted.
Day and night burneth the eternal lamp . . .
Whoever lighteth this lamp, to a high place doth he go.'

'In my own self have I found Him,' says the Master
Surdas Ji.

'The Sound Current giveth light and the Master showeth the
way.'

And Guru Arjan Dev writes:

'By linking with the Nam (Word) I saw immense lights
vying with millions of suns shining together.'

St. Augustine also speaks at some length of this experience.
He says:

'I entered even into my inward Self, Thou being my Guide,
and able I was for Thou wert become my Helper. And I
entered and beheld with the eye of my soul (such as it was),
above the same eye of my soul, above my mind, the Light
Unchangeable. Not this ordinary light which all flesh may
look upon, nor as it were a greater of the same kind, as
though the brightness of this should be manifold brighter,
and with its greatness take up all space. Not such was this
light, but other, yea, far other from all these . . . He that
knows the Truth knows what that light is, and he that knows
it knows Eternity.'

The last sentence of St. Augustine's statement is of special
interest, since it complements the saying of Jesus that:

'Ye shall know the truth and the truth shall make you free.'
John 8 : 32

The basic truth, the reality underlying all appearances, is
the Word or Holy Spirit, the Sound Current, which is the all

powerful and every where manifestation of God in action. It also is life and light, the power that created the light of the sun and the more brilliant lights of the heavenly worlds. St. Augustine, upon seeing the heavenly light, said, 'He that knows it knows eternity.' In other words, he has become freed of utter bondage to the body and the material world, his soul has begun to liberate itself from the clutches of the mind, and at long last is rising upwards towards its ultimate goal of complete freedom from all lower, material influences, the condition of its existence in its true home.

Some of the Masters have described in an arresting manner the difference between this world and the higher world that the student first enters after going within. This world, they say, is full of misery, selfishness, cruelty, greed, and other unpleasantness, and it is difficult to find any true happiness here. But if one goes within and rises up and tries to find misery, selfishness, or cruelty in the next higher world, it is impossible to find any of them there. In that world they simply do not exist.

The Master's Radiant Form

When the disciple reaches the astral realm he meets his own Master in his radiant form. This form is a higher form of the disciple's own Master, whom he knows and loves on the earth-plane. It resembles the Master's own physical form, but is exceedingly more beautiful and is radiant with the brilliant light of the spirit.

This meeting is comparable to the awe-inspiring revelation vouch-safed to a selected group of Jesus' disciples at the transfiguration.

The first form that the disciple sees is the astral form of the Master; but as he progresses he will see still higher and purer and more luminous radiant forms. When the highest heaven—

our true home—is reached, the being of the Master is one with the Supreme Father Himself.

Achievement of this inner meeting with the Master is made possible by a part of the divine plan of salvation that is almost totally unknown in the west. It is the fact that at the time of initiation the Master's omnipresent radiant form comes and stays within the disciple, in the third eye, which is the seat of the soul and the gateway to the higher worlds.

When the disciple succeeds in going within and his inner eyes are opened, he can finally see the inner light and at the same time the radiant form of the Master. To be sure, the radiant form is always with the disciple from the moment of his initiation, but the disciple cannot see it until by dint of faithful devotion to his daily meditation and the grace of the Master, his inner eye is opened. From that time on, the disciple can see the beloved Master in the inner or higher realms, as well as in the outer material world.

The inner meeting with the Master marks a most important turning point in the new birth and the life of the disciple. From that point on the whole course of his life is changed. For from that moment on the Master and the disciple are never separated until the Master has completed the work of bringing the disciple into the presence of his Father in heaven, the Supreme God of all other gods.

Jesus referred to the disciple's meeting with the radiant form of the Master when he said:

> 'He that hath my commandments and keepeth them, he it is that loveth me: and he that loveth me shall be loved of my Father, and I will love him, and *will manifest myself* to him.'
>
> *John 14 : 21*

If any disciple loves the Master and practises what he teaches him, he will surely enter the kingdom of light where

he will meet the Master in his radiant form. This is one part
of the spiritual birth that is a reward, or result, of faithful
practice. The Master always manifests himself to those who
love him and walk in his light. The radiant form of the
Master, moreover, is ubiquitous, omnipresent. It can be seen
at one and the same time by ten thousand or a hundred
thousand disciples.

Present-day disciples who have had this experience—and
there are many of them—will tell you that there is no joy in
this world so great as that which is experienced upon first
beholding the radiant Master. It is the culmination of many
lifetimes of struggle. It is the signal of victory in the long
battle with mind and matter. The disciple is then half way,
the Masters say, to the end of all his labours for spiritual
liberation. For the Master takes charge of the disciple, for the
rest of his spiritual journey.

In speaking again of the disciple's meeting with the Master
in his radiant form, Jesus says:

'Lo, I am with you always, even unto the end of the world.'
Matthew 28 : 20

This is a true description of the relationship between every
perfect Master and his disciples. Never again can the disciple
be alone or lonely. The Master is his friend, well-wisher, and
companion not only for life, but for eternity. Moreover, he
is a friend who continually pours out love transcending that
of any human being to each and every disciple. The Master
will never forsake or stop loving a disciple, even if the
disciple should forget or deny him.

A factor of great importance in this relationship is the fact
that the Master meets his disciples at the time of death and
goes with them when they leave this earth life. Wherever a
disciple may be, the Master comes to him in his radiant form
at some time before the end of his life and tells him that its

termination is near at hand. Then, as soon as the disciple leaves the physical body, the Master himself takes him to the heavenly region for which his progress on the path has fitted him. There, still under the Master's guidance, he continues his training until he is ready to go still higher.

This divine companionship is spoken of by Guru Nanak in the saying:

> 'O Nanak, break thou with false friends, and seek a perfect Sat Guru. The former part company in this very life, but the latter goes with thee even after death.'

As long as the disciple lives in the material world the Master is his truest friend and gives him instruction and guidance. Then, when he leaves this world, the Master in his astral form accompanies him still as friend and guide. Thus he never leaves the disciple until the final goal is reached. In the *Adi Granth* it is said:

> 'Devote yourself to the true Master and tune yourself to Nam (the Word). If you do so, the Master will receive you at the time of your departure from the body.'

It can now be seen that when one succeeds in going within the temple and thus entering the kingdom of heaven, the way is opened for the soul to begin the upward journey of its safe return, and all-powerful spiritual assistance is given to it.

Death has no more terrors for the man or woman who has been initiated and has learnt how to go within. People fear death because they do not know what it involves. The modern orthodox mind, moreover, is all too prone to say that what lies beyond the gates of death cannot be known—that it is a matter of faith and hope, not of provable facts.

But the Masters and their disciples know precisely what death is and what lies beyond it. They have themselves 'crossed the great divide' many times, and can speak not of what they believe, but of what they have already seen and known. This solves once and for all what is considered by many to be the most inexplicable problem that confronts human beings—the problem of death and what lies beyond it.

The great Master, Kabir Sahib, says:

> 'People are afraid of death, but I wait for it with joy.
> Oh, would that I might die soon, and go to my beloved Lord.'

The Masters of today, who know not only the meaning of death but also the meaning of eternal life, are ready to impart their knowledge to all who wish to listen to them. Not only this, but they are ready to show the sincere investigator just how he may acquire the same knowledge and how he may apply it to conquer death and gain immortal life.

With Jesus and the other Masters of all times, they say:

> 'I am the resurrection and the life. He that believeth in me, though he were dead, yet shall he live. And whosoever liveth and believeth in me shall never die.'

CHAPTER 12

AS YE SOW

'Whatsoever a man soweth, that shall he also reap.'
— *Galatians 6 : 7*

'Judge not, that ye be not judged. For with what judgement ye judge, ye shall be judged; and with what measure ye mete, it shall be measured to you again.'
— *Matthew 7 : 1-2*

In these words Jesus and the apostle Paul stated the law of karma, the immutable law of cause and effect that governs all human life and guides it towards its spiritual end.

Together with the law of karma, there goes hand in hand the related doctrine of reincarnation, the fact that each individual soul incarnates time after time in different bodies, returning to the material world again and again to spend many lifetimes here. In the east, this is called the wheel of births and deaths.

These two laws are so closely inter-related that they cannot be separated, for each one plays a part in the operation of the other. For the sake of clarity, however, they are discussed separately here.

The word 'karma' is derived from a Sanskrit root that means 'doing'. It is the law of doing or action, and the results of actions. In its operation it requires that every doer of actions shall receive an exact and unequivocally just reward or retribution for each and every one of his thoughts and actions, whether good or bad.

Good thoughts and actions means good karma, which

reveals itself in the form of happiness or good fortune of various kinds—material, mental, or spiritual—in the same or in future lives. Bad thoughts and actions imply bad karma, which must be paid for by experiencing equivalent unhappiness, pain, or suffering.

This is a law that nobody breaks, because nobody can break it. It is a law that is as certain in its operation as the law of gravity. Through the inexorable—but meticulously just—working of the karmic law, each individual reaps the results of his past deeds, whether good or bad, and harvests in the future the blessings or the disciplines produced by his present actions. The conditions of our present life, whether apparently good or bad, happy or unhappy, are the consequences of our own doings in the past.

Our thoughts and desires, whether pure or impure, rule our lives and also our destinies. As we think and desire, so we are and so we become. For thoughts and desires are things, and they follow the law of nature that like produces like. Our inmost thoughts and our heart's desires are our perpetual prayers, whether for good or ill; and the law of karma sees to it that these prayers are granted. Sooner or later we all sit down to a banquet of consequences.

In this connection, there are given here two fundamental principles which, according to the teachings of the Masters, explain what is basically wrong in thought or action, and what is fundamentally right. The first principle is:

Whatever bears the quality or character of any of the five evil passions—lust, anger, greed, attachment and vanity—or which in any way hinders or delays the soul in its progress towards spiritual freedom is wrong.

This is a certain guide to help the disciple to discriminate among his conflicting thoughts and emotions and to pick the thoughts or actions that will create good karma.

The second guiding principle is:

Whatever creates bad karma is wrong and whatever creates good karma is right.

In the last analysis, the law of karma is nothing more nor less than the law of cause and effect, with which everyone is familiar. Its underlying principle is the simple and logical one that every thought and act must be followed by its natural and legitimate results. The world which we do not see, the invisible world of thought, is the real world of causes. The world which we see around us is the world of effects. It is as essential to control our thoughts as it is to control our actions. For the thoughts that dwell habitually in our minds, and issue from us in speech and acts, determine our future happiness or unhappiness and our spiritual advancement or retrogression. We should try to govern our thoughts as if the whole world were able to read them.

Each day is like a furrow lying before us. Our thoughts, desires, and actions are the seeds that each minute we drop into it even though we do not perceive what seeds we are planting. When the furrow is completed, we commence upon another, then another and again another. Each day presents a fresh one, and so on to the end of life, sowing, ever sowing. And all we have sown springs up, grows, and bears fruit, either in this life or a succeeding one.

It may be mentioned here, however, that the law of karma holds sway only up to the region where mind and matter cease to operate. In the realms of mind and matter karma is universal. But, as has been pointed out, there is a higher universe of worlds where pure spirit reigns supreme and there is no karma there. It is to these worlds that the Master takes his disciples.

It is sometimes argued that a belief in the karmic law is fatalism, but nothing is farther from the truth. Fatalism is a lethargic condition in which people say of their misfortunes:

'It is the will of God. Of ourselves we can do nothing. The Deity has inflicted this adverse fate upon us.'

The law of karma, on the other hand, has shown us the path to freedom—*elcamino Real*. If a person has degraded himself by his bad thoughts and actions, it stands to reason that he will surely be able to lift himself up through the influence of his good thoughts and actions. If a man can bind himself to earth, he can most certainly unbind himself.

The law of karma, which may also be called the law of destiny, shows, as opposed to fatalism, that a man's destiny is the result of his own karmic actions. Thus man is the fashioner of his own fate. In doing this, he works in accordance with the divine plan for his own spiritual regeneration.

The law is not a blind force. It has a purpose to carry out, and that purpose is an educative and evolutionary one. We are here to learn—to learn that the purpose of human existence is spiritual progress; and the law helps us, sometimes forces us, to learn this lesson. The self-created experiences which we undergo are the lessons that will ultimately teach us. Often we learn unconsciously, without realising at the time, what is happening to us. But nevertheless we learn.

It is true that most of us seem to learn more from suffering than from pleasure. This is because we seldom learn enough from one single experience, no matter how bitter it may be. The lesson has to be repeated until it has been burnt into the heart and mind, and has been finally and irrevocably assimilated, and we have been purified by the refiner's fire. Our heartaches and struggles awaken us to truth and help us to grow. In the end we become aware of our true selves, realise that we are spiritual children of God, and understand that God's love has been the force that has been directing and guiding us. For love is the only force that the Supreme Father ever uses in carrying out His plan of redemption.

It is simply because of our ignorance of this inexorable law, and our failure to find any direct reason for our sufferings with our ordinary intelligence, that we sometimes tend to put all the blame on fate, or on an 'unjust' God, and regard Him as cruel or partial. We never for a moment reflect that we are suffering the consequences of our own past thoughts and actions. But the man of today is the product of his thoughts and actions of yesterday.

The average human being tends to attribute to God the evils that man does of his own free will. But God does not really need to punish us. We are ever busy creating our own punishment.

There is a divine plan at the back of all things, and it embraces each and every life. Our life is simply a spiritual education, and suffering caused by our past actions is a part of this. God has never deserted us, and whatever happens is for the ultimate spiritual evolution of the individual and of mankind. The worst experiences are sometimes means of bringing to pass unseen good, and the hardest sufferings have always a positive and constructive purpose behind them. And, like everything else in the material world, suffering cannot endure permanently. Sooner or later, it must come to an end, as night ends when dawn lightens the morning sky.

Within the framework of the law of karma we can learn that everywhere there is law and order. It is strange that in this scientific age, it is sometimes difficult to convince men that life is governed by law, as well as matter.

Many in the west are already familiar with the karmic law as a result of the widespread interest in recent years in the study of religions and philosophies of the east. It forms a part of practically all schools of oriental thought, and is accepted without question by more than half the human race.

As Jesus taught the law, he explained karma in the simplest terms as receiving what one has earned, or reaping what one has sown. If a farmer sows the seeds of wheat, he harvests wheat; but if he plants the seeds of thistles, he can logically and by the operation of a law of nature, expect nothing other than a crop of thistles. No one would look for any other result in the field of agriculture.

The law of karma operates in precisely the same way in the field of human affairs. If one plants the seeds of love, kindness, good will, just dealing, right conduct, and other good thoughts and actions, he will be repaid by receiving a welcome harvest of the same kind of treatment from others. But if his thoughts and deeds are those of anger, hatred, selfishness, cheating, or harming others and so on, he will become the victim of similar treatment meted out to him by karmic law through the instrumentality of others. His karmic debts must be paid, even though the theologians claim that another has paid for him.

In either case, the reward or penalty may be received in the present life or in some future life.

Says Guru Nanak:

'Our life is the farm where the seeds of karma are sown.'

In *The Light of Asia,* the story of the life and teachings of the Buddha, Sir Edwin Arnold describes the working of the karmic law with remarkable beauty, simplicity, and clarity.

'It will not be contemned of any one;
Who thwarts it loses, and who serves it gains;
The hidden good it pays with peace and bliss,
The hidden ill with pains.
It knows not wrath or pardon, utter-true
It measures mete, its faultless balance weighs;
Times are as nought, tomorrow it will judge,
Or after many days.
By this the slayer's knife did stab himself;
The unjust judge hath lost his own defender;

The false tongue dooms its lie; the creeping thief
And spoiler rob, to render.

Such is the law which moves to righteousness,
Which none at last can turn aside or stay;
The heart of it is Love, the end of it
Is Peace and Consummation sweet. Obey!

The Book says well, my Brothers! each man's life
The outcome of his former living is;
The bygone wrongs bring forth sorrows and woes,
The bygone right breeds bliss.

That which ye sow ye reap. See yonder fields!
The sesamum was sesamum, the corn
Was corn. The Silence and the Darkness knew
So is a man's fate born.'

Three Kinds of Karma

There are three kinds of karma recognised by the Masters:
fate, reserve and new.

Fate karma is that which has been created by actions in one
or more previous lives, and must be paid off in the present
life. There is no escape from it, as a rule, even if one has been
initiated by a living Master.

Reserve karma is the accumulated karma created during
many lifetimes, which has not yet been worked off. Only a
certain amount of karma is exhausted in each earthly existence,
and this is usually not sufficient to completely pay one's
karmic debts. What is not worked off is kept as reserve
karma. This karma is allotted as required by the lord of
karma.

An individual may, for example, work off all of the fate
karma allotted for a certain life. But this will not necessarily
free him from the wheel of births and deaths. The lord of
karma, who is Kal or the negative power, will immediately
burden the individual with some of his reserve karma.

New Karma is that which we are making now by our day-to-day thoughts and actions. We may work out all of this karma in the present life, or some of it may be added to our store of reserve karma. In the latter case, it will have to be worked off in the next life or some subsequent life.

It may be noted here that when a living Master initiates a disciple, he takes over from the negative power the administration of the disciple's karma. This is of incalculable benefit to the disciple, for it means that the Master will arrange matters so as to free him as rapidly as possible from the immense burden of karma accumulated during all of his past lives.

Our past actions cause our fate in this present life. They determine the general circumstances of our life, the nature of our family and home life, the environments into which we are born and into which we move as we grow older, and the major important events of our lives. In addition, past actions cause innate hopes and desires which are part of our very nature. These vary in enormous degree between different people. But in each case they drive the individual despite himself to think thoughts, experience desires, and perform actions that will make him experience the rewards or the penalties of past deeds, good and bad.

While we are thus working out the destiny which we have created for ourselves, we possess at the same time some free will, the power of choosing how we wish to think and act, and in this way shaping our future. It was our choice of what we would think and do in the past that created our present destiny. And so in this very life we can use our free will to shape a better future.

Many have been perplexed by the much-debated question: does man actually possess free will to choose, or are all his choices predetermined by his heredity and environment over which he has no control? The answer is that he does possess limited free will and that it is one of his most precious possessions. For, when rightly used, it is a major factor in his evolution towards his ultimate spiritual destiny. If man could control and direct his will, he would become the conscious creator of his future karma and therefore, in the popular phrase, the master of his destiny.

If men, on the other hand, forget their higher selves and choose to satisfy their material and animal desires, they are free to do so. But they reap what they sow. If, on the other hand, they choose to lead an upright life as best they can and to look inward and listen to the 'still, small voice' of conscience that God has implanted in them, they will slowly but surely rise towards spirituality.

The divine plan for our redemption calls for gradual but certain awakening as the result of karmic experiences and the impact of these experiences on the choices that we make regarding the conduct of our life. It operates in simple accordance with the principles that experience is the best teacher, and that human experience shapes human character.

When the law of karma is correctly understood, it becomes clear that each event, experience or set of circumstances caused by a past action has the purpose of enabling the individual to learn from experience, from his past mistakes. If the lesson is not learnt the first time, it is inevitably repeated. Through such lessons the individual is powerfully helped to overcome weaknesses, faults, wrong attitudes or materialistic ideas that are impeding his spiritual progress.

Some heed the warnings quickly. Others pay no regard to them. But after repeated 'blows of fate', which actually are the results of similar blows that we have dealt to others in times past, one begins to learn.

When one finally sees clearly, beyond any possibility of doubt, that a wrong action committed today must be paid for, either in this life or a later one, it is the strongest possible deterrent to a repetition of similar deeds. Suffering brought about by karmic law is a powerful and persuasive teacher. Pain is the hard coin we are forced to pay for wisdom. It is in this way that we finally reach the state of possessing 'a humble and a contrite heart', and in the end we give unstinted and joyous thanks for every moment of purifying suffering through which we have passed.

And it must never be forgotten that karma includes the good, as well as the bad, the boon of happy days and years as well as the rigours of mental or physical sickness or pain. If one earns the good, he must and will get the good. Nothing can possibly defeat the law and prevent it from coming to him.

When we realise that everything, good or bad, that comes to us has been previously earned or created by ourselves alone, we will know that we must not hold anybody else responsible for anything that we suffer. We all have a tendency to blame others for whatever in our life may go wrong. But if we are ready to assume responsibility for our own karmic debts, and not accuse others, then it will be easier for us to forgive those who willingly or unwillingly hurt us or do us some harm. For we will realise that they are being used as instruments by the lord of karma, and that whatever they have done to us is the result of some similar past action of our own.

The basic purpose of the karmic law is to goad us into making spiritual progress. He who starts today merely takes the step that others will have perforce to take tomorrow. Man is created in the image of God and, by the Creator's divine plan, is relentlessly impelled towards the ultimate achievement of Godlikeness. Self-improvement is what we are in the world for. It is our first and most sacred duty. And the disciple soon learns what is true for him and all others, that not one effort is wasted, not one struggle fails to advance him, and that every effort to do the right thing carries him forward on the path of spiritual progress.

Every spiritual desire or aspiration goes on and obeys a higher law. It is never lost. It does not matter if you do not see immediate results. They will come to you in due time, as incalculable blessings. The result of every fine and noble thought has far-reaching effects, and you will know one day that the faintest longing for the higher life has helped you towards spiritual liberation.

What is the ultimate purpose of the karmic law? It is to purify the individual and to bring him in the end to a living Master, who will free him of his karmic debts and take him back to his spiritual home. This is the greatest good fortune that can come to any man or woman, the very highest reward for acting in such a manner as to create good karma.

For, when the Master is met, an early liberation from the wheel of births and deaths and the pain and suffering of human life is assured. At the time of initiation the Master takes over the responsibility of the disciples karmic account from the negative power. This is one of the greatest acts of love that the Master does for His followers. Thereafter, the Master arranges for the working out of the disciple's karmic debts, and does so with infinite kindness and mercy, lightening the burden as much as is possible.

The Master then leads the disciple through meditation to the higher realms, which are beyond the jurisdiction of the negative power and the karmic law. The path of salvation, the path of the safe return to the soul's true home, then lies open before him, stretching away to the ever-higher spiritual realms and illuminated by the light of the Word and the radiance of the Master's constant presence.

CHAPTER 13

IF YE WILL RECEIVE IT

'And if ye will receive it, this is Elias, which was for to come.'

—Matthew 11 : 14

From what has been said concerning karma, it can be seen that more than one lifetime is necessary for the working out of our many past acts and for the gradual process of purification which leads us at last to the Master, and through him to God-consciousness and the kingdom of God.

Reincarnation is called in the east *awagawan,* or 'coming and going'. It is the ages-long succession or 'wheel' of births and deaths through which every soul must pass on its way to ultimate perfection and divinity. So long as the individual lives in the lower worlds under the jurisdiction of the law of karma, he cannot escape this coming and going.

Only a perfect living Master can bring to an end this weary series of lives, during each of which the immortal soul of man is imprisoned in a gross body and deluded by the mind and senses.

That Jesus was thoroughly conversant with the operation of the law of karma is evidenced by his sayings. There is no doubt, moreover, that he was equally familiar with the law of reincarnation. This may sound dogmatic, since reincarnation is not a doctrine of the present-day Christian church; but it is not intended to be so. It is a simple fact that every Master knows of this law and can see how it operates, from the vantage point of the higher worlds.

Actually, the history of religions shows that reincarnation is one of the most ancient doctrines, and is still regarded as an inseparable and logically necessary part of religion by many more human beings than the number of those who know not of it or who deny it.

It was explained in detail in the sacred scriptures of early India, which are still revered today by modern Indians. It was taught by the noblest philosophers of Greece. The millions of Buddhists throughout the east, in China, Japan, Burma, Thailand, Ceylon, and other countries, now believe in reincarnation as did their forefathers before them. The Mohammedan saints believed in it and spoke of it to their followers. 'Again and again we have been born like grass in the green meadows,' says Maulana Rum. 'Many lives and countless bodies we have seen.' It formed a part of the Jewish religion, and it has not disappeared from that faith. And Jesus also believed and taught it. It was known and taught in the early Christian church, and was promulgated by the most revered leaders of the church.

Jesus, it should be remembered, was himself a Jew and consequently was entirely familiar with the doctrines believed by the Jews. One of these was reincarnation. For them, Moses, Adam, Noah, Seth, and others had returned to earth, and during the lifetime of Jesus it was believed that the prophet Elias (the Greek form of Elijah) was yet to return.

In his own teachings, in the partial record of them that we have today, Jesus never denies the doctrine of reincarnation. To the contrary, he clearly believed and taught it when he said that John the Baptist was actually the Elias of former times whom the people were expecting.

'And if ye will receive it, this is Elias, which was for to come.'

Matthew 11 : 14

'I say unto you, that Elias is come already, and they knew him not.'

Matthew 17 : 12

From the words, 'If ye will receive it,' it seems apparent that at the time of Jesus' ministry, even as today, many were doubtful regarding the truth of reincarnation. This is quite possible and was doubtless due to the work of the religious authorities and the priests. For at all times the priests have arranged matters so that they could retain the power to threaten individuals with dire punishments in the after-life. And if all men were thoroughly familiar with the karmic law and reincarnation, the power of the priests to frighten people would be either lessened or destroyed. For the people would then know beyond the shadow of a doubt that their punishments come from themselves alone.

Following Jesus, the apostle Paul spoke of Esau and Jacob as having lived before; and later such great Christian leaders as Origen, Synesius and others, believed in and taught that reincarnation was a fact. John the revelator says in Revelations 3 : 12, that he was told in a vision that whosoever should overcome the material world would no longer be under the necessity of 'going out' from the kingdom of heaven. That is, he would no longer need to be reincarnated and pass through other lives in the lower worlds.

Thus, for several centuries after the time of Jesus the belief in reincarnation was part of Christianity. As time went on, however, disputes arose and there were many controversies concerning which of the sayings of Jesus were authentic and which should be included in the New Testament.

It must be remembered when reading a book like the New Testament that it contains many interpolations, additions, mistranslations, and even misrepresentations. It was not until several centuries after Jesus' death that certain books were collected by a self-elected council and compiled as the New

Testament. Other books concerning Jesus and his teachings were arbitrarily rejected by this council.

During its sessions, there was much heated and bitter controversy regarding which books and sayings were accurate reports of what had actually been taught by the Master. Some men insisted that reincarnation should be included in the doctrine of Christianity. They would not have done this if they had not been justified by some of the recorded sayings and teachings of Jesus. These early church leaders, however, were in the minority, and as a result the doctrine of reincarnation was rejected, and references to it made by Jesus were not permitted to appear in the New Testament.

The church, in arguing on the doctrine, put forward the objection that if men were convinced that they would live many times, the temptation to accept the present apparent state of things and indulge in the sensual and other pleasures of the world, without striving for higher things, would be too strong. But actually, what stronger reason could there be for abstaining from actions that we know to be wrong, than the positive knowledge that each evil action of any kind will without fail cause us to suffer? A thorough understanding of reincarnation and karma is the most powerful force that will make men pursue in fact the ethical conduct that they know about in theory.

The laws of karma and reincarnation provide the only rational explanation for many things that have puzzled thinking persons throughout the centuries, and that still puzzle many of today.

Why, for example, are some children born into wealthy families and others into poor ones? Why do some people have noble, aspiring characters from childhood on, while others are dishonest, crafty, and self-seeking? Why do some older people of apparently low intelligence linger on, burdens to themselves and everyone else, while a beautiful child, full of promise and joy, dies at an early age? Why are some born healthy and sound, while others have some physical or mental handicap or suffer much from illness during their lives? Why are some children born with superior intelligence, while others are hopelessly dull?

All these disparities among people in respect to their characters, capabilities, environments, health, and so on, are results of karma, the consequences of past thoughts, desires, and actions. Only karma and reincarnation provide any rational and truly satisfactory explanation. The differences in the lives and fortunes of different people are not due to arbitrary decrees of deity or an inscrutable 'will of god'. They are due to the fate which each one of us has shaped for himself.

Take the case of the child who dies at an early age, leaving the parents stricken with grief. To many, this seems one of the cruelest blows that 'fate' can deal. In such a case, it must be understood that the child was from the beginning allotted just that brief span of earth life, owing to his or her own past karma. When the allotted time was finished, the child had to leave the earth life.

For the parents, moreover, the birth and short life of the child, together with the grief felt at its departure, was also a karmic episode brought into their lives by some past event. Karma of some kind had to be paid or balanced off between all three of the persons involved. When it was paid, the episode was closed and a karmic debt of some kind was partially or wholly wiped out. And through their sorrow, perhaps, one or both of the parents gained deeper understanding or compassion, or were driven to seek more ardently for the spiritual path.

Or take the much more common case of an unhappy marriage that ends in separation or divorce, leaving both husband and wife in a state of bitterness. The marriage took place because there was a karmic debt of some nature to be paid off, or a karmic lesson for both to learn.

In life after life we have tried to find true happiness. We have sought it in wealth, in fame, in sense pleasures, and in many other material and worldly ways. In life after life we have been absorbed in our struggles, our hopes, our fears, and our aspirations.

But unaware of the true purpose underlying our existence, the true objective of our lives on earth, we have spent our time in stumbling and groping. All of these activities have created karma and have brought us to the point at which we stand today. And we will continue in the same blind and ignorant fashion until we create enough good karma to bring us to a living Master. He will then release us from reincarnation forever.

It has been emphasised many times that the teachings of the Masters are a spiritual science, and that the Masters' followers can prove for themselves the truth of every statement made. This is true of the laws of karma and reincarnation, as with everything else. Final and conclusive proof comes when, guided by the Master, one enters the higher worlds and sees there for himself the operation of karma and reincarnation in his life and in the lives of others. When one makes some progress on the path, this becomes possible.

At that stage everyone is able to see clearly his own past lives, and it is then that he knows without any possibility of doubt that he has lived before. He knows, moreover, just where and when he has lived, and he learns of his own karmic gains and losses. He can see exactly how the laws of karma and reincarnation have worked out in his long succession of lives, and how he has suffered and enjoyed according to his debits and credits. The great law of karma is then no mere theory, but a fact verified by direct knowledge and realisation.

Before a disciple reaches this stage he may find more than satisfactory confirmation of karma and reincarnation from eye-witness accounts given to him by fellow disciples more advanced than himself. From time to time, the Masters, for one good purpose or another, give advanced disciples permission to tell others of their experiences in the higher worlds.

There is only one reason why we are here on earth, and that is to work our way upward until our good karma makes us fit to meet a living Master and through his help return to our original home. Until we succeed in this we come back again and again. But when this happens, we have reached the supreme goal of all human life. Our early and final liberation from the trials, tribulations, and tragedies of life in the material world is then assured.

Today there is a better opportunity than for many centuries for the Masters to obtain a hearing, for more people have reached the point of being ready for them. When still more people are ready for them, more Masters will come, in different parts of the world. No enlightenment can possibly take place until the people are sufficiently awakened to listen to the teacher; and they do not become sufficiently awakened until their karmic experiences have made them so.

For age after age the higher faculties are drugged by the mind and the senses. Men live the life of animals, and their clever worldly minds supply well-reasoned justification for such a life. A Master could shout his divine message into their ears, and it would only annoy them. They do not want to be disturbed. They will pay no heed to a Master, or may even drive him away or kill him, as everyone knows has happened in the past.

Until men reach a certain stage of enlightenment, they simply cannot hear or do not want to hear what a Master has to say. They are engrossed in one form or another of material or mental activity, and the spiritual instincts are suppressed or covered over by these surface interests. It is only a waste of time for a Master to even attempt to enlighten them. And that is the chief reason why the great Masters have not been able to give their message to the whole world. They simply could not do it. The people would not accept it.

The mills of God grind slowly, but they grind exceedingly fine. These mills are the mills of karma and reincarnation. Age after age the karmic millstones grind and purify the minds of men, and in the end all true spiritual seekers will see the light and will run with rejoicing hearts and outstretched hands to meet it.

CHAPTER 14

BORN OF THE SPIRIT

*'That which is born of the Spirit is spirit. Marvel not
that I said unto thee, Ye must be born again.'*
                                        —John 3 : 6-7

*'Verily, verily, I say unto thee, Except a man be born
again, he cannot see the kingdom of God.'*
                                        —John 3 : 3

The second or spiritual birth of a human being is the most
important event of his entire series of earthly existences. It
is the goal towards which he has constantly been progressing,
albeit much of the time unconsciously, throughout all his
lives in the material world.

When one is born of the Spirit, his prodigal wanderings in
the dark worlds of matter and ignorance are at an end. The
divine and other-worldly soul, so long held a captive, is
finally freed from the clutches of the mind, the senses and the
five evil passions, and is able to rise up and begin the return
to its true home.

Once we begin to walk on the path of the Masters, we
begin to tread the path of our true destiny, and travel with joy
and certainty towards the radiant kingdom that ultimately all
will reach.

This is salvation, the safe return to the Father's house. The
Masters not only give this gift to the disciple, but set definite
time limits for its achievement. When an individual is initiated,
it is certain that he will gain liberation or salvation within a
few lifetimes. Many, to be sure, reach the end of the path—

the highest heavenly region—in a shorter length of time. But all, without any exception, will attain the goal within the space of a few lifetimes.

Initiation Is The First Step

The first step in being born anew is initiation by a living perfect Master, at which time the Master connects the soul with the Word, the all-powerful current of spiritual life. One great Indian Master, as has already been said, called the initiation and what follows thereafter, 'the science of connecting the individual soul with its Creator'.

At the time of initiation the seed of the spiritual life is planted in the disciple and, like a material seed, it must and will grow and bring forth fruit. The process is in accordance with natural and spiritual law, and the result is inevitable. Thereafter, as the soul is drawn upward by the power of the Audible Life Stream and rises above the body consciousness, it comes in due time into cosmic awareness and the spiritual birth is brought to a state of ultimate perfection. Initiation means the beginning of a new and higher life, a new and broader outlook, and a new and deeper understanding.

Volumes have been written about the second birth referred to by Jesus, but its true and specific nature is still a matter of obscurity to most people in the west. In some way it is supposed to be performed by the Holy Spirit. But what takes place and how it takes place is no more than a vague surmise.

The Masters, however, can and do explain the nature and meaning of the spiritual birth. They know exactly what it consists of. For the Masters throughout human history have been the divinely appointed agents of the Supreme Father sent to this planet to give the new birth to those who long for it in right earnest and are ready for it.

This they can do because they have free access to the souls

of men. Their revivifying spiritual power and love can therefore pierce through the outer coverings, and reach and teach the soul within by direct communication between soul and soul.

Speaking of this fact, the Master Sawan Singh Ji says:

'Saints, if they like, may pass their magnetism to others. Through word, touch or look, they may use their power. They may not use the external organs and, instead, may use the mind or even the soul, and affect the mind or soul of the other, without the other person even being made aware of it. These latter ways are the rule rather than the exception.'

The power of the Masters to reach the soul is of the utmost importance, for in this way they can contact and bring to light the God-power within ourselves. The Masters can ignore or bypass the mind and exert their spiritualising power directly on the soul. Thus they gradually develop or liberate a soulforce within us of which we were not previously aware, and which in time becomes the dominant factor in our lives.

It is difficult to realise, but human life on this earth is death, as compared to the life of radiant purity, bliss, and spirituality of the higher worlds. Over and over again the Masters have referred to the physical birth as a death, because it means that the soul, bright and radiant from God in its essential nature, must once again go down into darkness. When the soul leaves any of the higher regions and comes down to the world of matter, it means descent into darkness and relative death.

Says Hazrat Inayat Khan:

'He who depends upon his (physical) eyes for sight, his ears for hearing, and his mouth for speech, he is still dead.'

The real birth takes place when the soul is connected with

the great luminous reality of the Sound Current or Holy Spirit by a perfect Master.

Thus, initiation is the first step in the divinely planned process that releases man from the relative death of the physical world and makes it possible for him to awaken spiritually, or be born of the spirit, and then rise up to live the spiritual and infinitely joyous life of the higher realms from which he long ago descended. There is but one final proof that this is true, one supreme authority by which it can be proved beyond dispute. And this is the authority of one's personal experience, one's own first-hand realisation that it is a verifiable fact. This realisation is made possible through initiation by a perfect Master and by the practice of meditation in which these Masters instruct their disciples.

The modern western world believes that it has little use for meditation. But those who think it a waste of time to attend to spiritual meditation before they have taken care of their worldly affairs put second things first and first things second.

Spiritual advancement is not a casual or haphazard affair but a steady and regular effort, and daily meditation, in accordance with the instructions of the Master, is the age-old and oft-proven way to such advancement. Such meditation, together with the unstinted help given by the Master, leads in the end to a change in the disciple's life that is little short of the miraculous.

All the Masters say to their disciples, as did Jesus to his closest followers:

'It is given unto you to know the mysteries of the kingdom.'
Matthew 13 : 11

This is not a theory. It is an actual fact, which each and every disciple finds to be true as he progresses on the path.

The essential meaning of birth is a bringing out into the light. This is exactly what the new birth does. Once the soul has been connected by the Master with the heavenly music of the Holy Spirit and the disciple has learnt how to listen day after day to its sublime and uplifting strains, he is gradually drawn up by it into the realms of light.

Jesus speaks of the Word or Sound Current when he says:

> 'That which is born of Spirit is spirit.' (the Holy Spirit or divine Sound Current).
>
> *John 3 : 6*

The spirit, or the Holy Spirit, as has already been said many times, is the sacred and sublime Sound Current , the stream of love and power that emanates continuously from the Supreme Father, maintaining at all times a connection with Him. Thus, Jesus points out in this statement that the spirit or soul of man is born anew and enabled to begin to grow to its full maturity and splendour by the action of the Holy Spirit in the form of the Sound Current or Audible Life Stream.

There can be no new birth without the power of the Sound Current or Holy Spirit, and the current cannot be contacted until one has first found a living Master who can 'tune him in' with it.

Then, just as the new-born baby grows gradually into a child, then a young man, and then comes slowly to old age, so does the soul grow gradually in the knowledge of the higher worlds. Initiation is the supreme moment of its new birth. But the completion of that birth is usually a slow process, a very gradual coming into the light.

A man is neither good nor wise all at once. He slowly betters himself, with the help and guidance of the Master, and gradually ascending, he at last reaches the summit of human and spiritual achievement.

The glorious melodies of the Divine Sound cannot be heard by the physical ears. They are heard at first by the ear of our inner body, and this the Master begins to open at the time of initiation. It is a celestial, spiritual music and a heavenly light so subtle and of such a high vibration that it cannot be detected by the physical senses. Nor can it be adequately described in human language.

Says the *Adi Granth:*

'Without eyes is it seen, and without ears is it heard.'

The Word, says Guru Nanak, is sweet beyond description. It is veritably the nectar of immortality, for if we drink it, it will make us immortal. While pleasures of the world entangle us in the wheel of births and deaths, the Word liberates us from the wheel and bestows immortality. To one who has tasted this nectar, all pleasures of the world seem insipid and of no worth whatever.

While a disciple of a perfect Master may hear the heavenly music resounding loud and clear, it cannot be heard by others who have not been initiated. Says Maulana Rum:

'Within himself hundreds of voices doth he hear; but of these even the man next to him getteth not an inkling.'

But even a disciple must attain to a certain degree of purity before he can hear the Sound Current in all of its power, beauty, and glory. Maulana Rum points out this truth, saying:

'Thine ear those Melodies does not hear, for by evil deeds hath it been polluted.'

After initiation or the spiritual birth, however, the Master aids the disciple by using many and various subtle and powerful means to purify his mind and deliver it from bondage to the senses and the attractions of the material world.

'Like God, without organs doth the Guru act; and without speaking doth he give lessons to his disciples,' says Maulana Rum.

The great nineteenth-century Indian Saint, Soami Ji Maharaj of Agra says in the *Sar Bachan*:

> 'Those who wish to enjoy the bliss of Nam (the Word or the Sound Current) in their spiritual practices should give up all other practices and firmly take refuge in the Sat Guru, who is all-powerful, and will make this human being pure and whole. That is, he will cleanse his mind, which is now filled with desires for sensual enjoyments, and soiled with the filth of lust, anger, greed, attachment, and egotism. He will also remove the infirmities and sickness on account of which the human being cannot taste the sweetness of Nam (the Sound Current), and will also bestow that Bliss upon Him.'

Furthermore, when the disciple begins to hear the Sound Current, its spiritual music also acts to purify the mind and soul until at last all evil deeds of the past and the karma they have created are washed away.

Guru Nanak expressed this by using a homely and easily understandable simile. He said:

> 'When clothes get dirty, they are washed with soap; when the mind is polluted with sins, by Nam it is washed.'

As the Holy Spirit gradually interpenetrates the whole being of the disciple, he begins to find out who and what he really is. Little by little he comes to know that he is not a prisoner of the body, not a captive enmeshed in the network of never-ceasing thoughts, and not a hapless victim of the fleeting passions. Slowly and by gentle stages he begins to discover that in reality he is a being that is purely and eternally divine—the immortal spiritual self.

Under the subtle and powerful spiritual influence of the Word, the disciple throws off without effort the petty and the personal, and discovers his illimitable and divine nature. The attractions of the world which previously occupied all his waking thoughts begin to melt away and disappear. The Sound Current, flooding his inner being with its beauty and spiritual power, carries him beyond the realm of intellect and lifts him up to the worlds of eternal light, beauty, and reality. For this he was really born, and not merely to go through the routine round of daily toil and domestic life. And this is the inevitable result of being born anew and of the spirit.

The New Birth and Karma

It can be seen that initiation by a living perfect Master brings with it very definite and vital evidence of the nature and reality of the new birth of the spirit or soul.

But there is still another way in which the boundless love of the Master helps his disciples to achieve the goal of spiritual freedom.

At the time of initiation the Master takes over from the negative power the karmic accounts—the karmic debits and credits—of the disciple. From the moment that the Master takes charge of the soul, the karmic cycle of cause and effect at once and forever begins to come to an end. From that moment on it is the Master who administers the working out of the disciple's karma, the paying of the debts incurred during his past and present lives. Gradually, and with infinite love and mercy, the Master enables the disciple to wind up all his karmas and thus escape for ever from the necessity of returning to the earth plane.

The reserve karma, representing the accumulated and unpaid karmic debts of innumerable earlier lives, is gradually 'burnt away' by the power of the Sound Current. The process is compared to that of putting seeds in a pan and placing it over a fire. The heat then causes the seeds to puff up and lose their ability to grow again.

As a rule, part of the new karma that the disciple has

created in the present life has already been settled in this life before the time of initiation. With regard to the remainder, the Master first teaches the disciple how to act so as to produce no additional karma. This is achieved by making one's best effort to decide what to do and what not to do; by weeding out imperfections through daily study and analysis; and by acting always in the name of the Master, acting as his instrument or agent. This will, of necessity, oblige him to do only what he believes the Master will approve. At the same time, the Master may arrange a general clemency with regard to the wrong deeds done in the earlier part of the present life.

Acting always in the name of the Master or acting as his agent, is a way of living that creates almost no new karma at all. If the Master's disciple wishes to escape the creation of karma of any kind, let him always act as the Master's agent as he goes about his daily activities. As long as he does this, he will not create new karma, because he is acting solely as the agent of another, and it is a law that the principal is responsible for the acts of his agents.

But the disciple must do this not merely in a surface manner, but with his entire heart, mind, and soul. In deepest earnest, let him do all things, every detail of his business, personal, and social life, in the name of his Master. This will, of necessity, oblige him to do only what he thinks the Master will approve. Then, essentially, it is the Master acting, not the disciple.

The fate karma, which was allotted for the present life, is not touched by the Masters. It is like an arrow shot into the air, which cannot be called back. The disciple must experience whatever of good or bad has been preordained for him in this present earth existence. There is, however, a vast difference in the amount of pain or pleasure experienced by a disciple who has made some measure of progress on the spiritual path and the experience of one who has not entered on the path.

Disciples who can go within and upward to a certain extent are better able than others to cope with bodily or mental pains and the worldly anxieties, fears, and hopes caused by their fate karmas for this life.

With regard to all the disciple's karmas, the Master always acts with boundless love and mercy and in accordance with what he knows is best for the disciple. He may require the disciple to work out all of his reserve karma. On the other hand, he may, out of his great love, bear a portion of this and other karmas himself. Whatever course is followed, the Master never permits the burden to become too heavy.

This is one of the incalculable benefits of discipleship.

CHAPTER 15

THROUGH THE WORD

'Now ye are clean through the word which I have spoken unto you.'

—John 15 : 3

There is little doubt that in the above quotation, as in a number of others, either the translation or the interpretation of Jesus', original words is incorrect. As translated, the statement refers to words that Jesus spoke. Actually, however, Jesus used the term 'Word', meaning the Word of God or the Audible Life Stream.

Knowing that Jesus was in contact with the Sound Current and taught it to his initiated disciples, it is probable that he actually said: 'Now ye are clean through the Word of which I have spoken unto you.'

In this statement Jesus spoke of the purifying power of the Word. This is one of the major means by which the Sound Current plays a part of great importance in liberating the soul from the material world and helping it to rise. It cleanses the mind of the lower desires. It is the Sound Current or Holy Spirit alone that has the power to finally and completely bring the mind to heel and wash it clean of evil tendencies. The mind can be fully controlled only by a power that has its origin beyond the mind, and that is the Divine Sound, which emanates from the highest realms of pure spirituality.

Men can struggle their hardest to purify the mind and forget the desires, distractions and sense pleasures of the world, but they simply cannot uproot and finally get rid of their desires without the aid of the spiritual purifying power of the Sound Current. The Word, or Holy Spirit, alone can subdue the worldly passions and bring about the supremacy of the spirit over the flesh. It is the supreme purifying agent of this and all worlds.

The Indian Master, Soami Ji of Agra, stated this truth very explicitly when he said:

> 'By listening to the Sound Current is the mind controlled;
> it yields not to a million efforts. By listening to the Sound
> Current alone is it controlled.'

And in the *Adi Granth*, the scripture of the Sikh religion, it is written:

> 'Shabd burneth all desire, and Guru's devotee findeth light
> within him.'

When the soul is brought into contact with the powerful and purifying music of the Sound Current by a perfect Master, it is drawn up to higher spheres, and all lower tendencies are wiped out. The five passions or enemies of man—lust, anger, greed, attachment, and egotism—are driven out by the transcendent melody. Thus it is only by listening to the divine strains of the Audible Life Stream that we can finally overcome all temptations and become truly pure in heart. It is the supreme essential in the liberation of every soul.

Says Shams-i-Tabriz:

> 'The Music of His love cometh all of a sudden, and from the
> clutches of greed and lust doth it liberate thee.'

When this high and other-worldly music is contacted and heard day after day, it begins to transfigure a man's entire nature. It reveals to him a divine infinitude and a secret splendour within himself. Slowly but surely he is freed of the petty and the personal, and becomes conscious of his divine and illimitable nature. As he continues to be absorbed in the sublime and soul-absorbing melody, the fascinations of the material world begin to melt away and lose their glamour, and he commences to discover his true self, the immortal soul, which is a spark of the divine light.

Magnetic Power of the Word

In addition to being the supreme purifying power, the Sound Current is the great attractive or magnetic power by which the Supreme Father draws us up, frees us from the limitations and impurities of this world, and brings us safely back at last to our eternal home. This power that comes from God is the same power that takes us back to God.

The Sound Current has two aspects, a centrifugal flow and a centripetal flow. It radiates outward from God, and it flows back towards God. Moving upon the current, all life and all power appear to flow outwards to the uttermost bounds of creation, and again upon it all life appears to be returning to its source. It is the second aspect of the current with which the disciples of a Master have mostly to deal, for it is upon the current's return flow to God that they depend for their return to their original home.

It will be remembered that the original meaning of the word 'religion' is to bind the soul back to God. The Sound Current is the one and only thing in the world that can and does do this. And, since it binds us to God, it is the one and only *real* religion. When it has been found and contacted, everything else in the field of religion will be only a substitute or a symbolic representation of the inner spiritual reality, the Holy Spirit of God.

Maulana Rum, speaking of the Sound Current's magnetic power says:

'If even an inkling of those Melodies do I give thee, then
would thy dead soul rise from its grave.'

The grave of the soul is the human body. The soul is, so
to speak, buried in the body; but the Sound Current has the
power to draw it up out of its earthly grave as a magnet
attracts a needle. Through the divine Word the soul, the 'bird
of heaven', can be freed from the cage of the physical frame
and can regain the freedom of the spiritual life and its eternal
home. Since in essence the soul and the Sound Current are
one, both being pure spirit, the current draws the soul upward
through the attraction of like for like. By listening to its
transcendent music, God is truly known, and then all external
worship seems futile.

This fact, that souls can work out their salvation only if
they come into contact with a perfect Master and learn from
him the secret of the Word is not, it should be remembered,
a new thing. It has been known, and known to many,
throughout all the ages of the world's history. It may sound
new to some in the west, but that is of no consequence. The
truth of its existence and power remains, and remains forever.

Enduring Happiness

As the spiritual strains of the Sound Current draw up the soul,
the disciple at last begins to understand the meaning of true
and enduring happiness. For he at long last is able to become
absorbed in the soul-satisfying bliss of the diviner states
which are open to him and to all mankind. The treasure of the
Word is inexhaustible. It gives to mortals the highest, purest,
and most intense happiness and bliss.

Even before a man or woman becomes a disciple there is
usually a deep felt realisation of the fact that genuine happiness
is not to be found in the sense indulgences, nor even in the
higher satisfactions of the mind. All pleasures of the senses,

and even those of the mind, are transitory and ephemeral. They are not lasting. For a moment they endure, and then they are gone. Nothing that is earthly can ever really satisfy. Moreover, there is rarely any unalloyed happiness in this world. All human enjoyment is tinged with sadness. Only too often do the short-lived worldly pleasures come to an end in bitterness and misery.

The pleasures of this world may often seem sweet, but their reactions are often bitter. There is only one pleasure, one bliss, that involves no reaction, and that is the bliss of the supreme and supernal Word.

True peace and happiness, we slowly learn, do not come from outer conditions, but from within. When we contact the Sound Current, we are able to gain from within the happiness which previously we always sought from without. For by listening to the Voice of God we are drawn ever closer to the condition of sublime and radiant joy in which the real self and the Supreme Father continually abide.

Unfailing happiness based on certain knowledge comes to us through this conscious realisation of God and of His presence within us. On that we can rely with the utmost confidence.

The *Adi Granth* says:

> 'In the union of the soul with Shabd is happiness; in the realisation of the Almighty Lord is bliss'.
> 'In bliss am I, for Shabd hath my Guru manifested within me. Anhad Bani raineth the nectar of bliss, and giveth peace to mind and body.'

And in a typically colourful description of the joy experienced by all who hear the heavenly music, Khwaja Hafiz says:

> 'If our Musician (God) singeth but one tune, into ecstasy and dancing would fall the pious priests.'

Guru Nanak reiterated the same truth when he said:

> 'All Creation is miserable; only he is happy who is in contact with the Word.'

> 'The Voice of God resounds from the vault of the temple (the human body), but the sleepy world hears it not. Oh! multitude! who remain deaf to His calling, behold the happiness of the few spiritually awakened, who listen to the Voice of the Lord and are joined to Him.'

Jesus spoke of this higher and never-failing happiness when he told his disciples:

> 'These things have I spoken unto you, that my joy might remain in you, and that your joy might be full.'
>
> *John 15 : 11*

And on another occasion he told his hearers:

> 'Blessed are they that hear the Word of God, and keep it.'
>
> *Luke 11 : 28*

All the great Masters are serene and joyous in the highest possible sense, since all of them are filled with the radiant light, love, and joy of the Word. And to be filled with this joy is true religion. For that alone is true religion which enables the soul to discover and consciously take part in the eternal and blissful joy of the infinite.

For all who have to live amid the manifold pressures and anxieties of today, the spiritual Yoga of the Masters offers a way that leads to ever greater inner peace and deep abiding happiness. The path of the Masters leads to the growth of spiritual power, but at the same time it gives far greater power for serene, harmonious, and truly care-free living. The way of life and the spiritual practice taught by the perfect Masters of the Word are, in fact, the most intensely practical bases of human existence. Their gifts are peace of mind and quietness of heart, higher guidance to solve the problems of daily living, the divine inner companionship of the beloved Master at all times and seasons, and daily contact with the joyous and uplifting power of the Holy Spirit or Sound Current.

Once you have placed yourself in the hands of the Master and the Holy Spirit, a higher life has begun. Inwardly there will be an abiding tranquillity and serene happiness never known before, even though outwardly life may still be less than perfect. You cannot care more for your affairs than the Master and the Holy Spirit of God care for you. And the spiritual science of the Masters brings you both the Master and the Holy Spirit.

When the spiritual Sound Current is once contacted, life ceases to be a dull and plodding affair, and becomes infused with a divine exultation. The disciple then knows that life can never again descend to monotony or the common-place. Even at the beginning there come memorable moments when the disciple experiences glimpses of the higher existence possible to man. He knows then that the soul's highest aspirations can come true, that love and peace and happiness are indeed his birthright.

When the student reaches the higher spiritual worlds—and many thousands of present-day men and women who are disciples of the Masters have done so—he possesses true beatitude. For God, flowing with boundless love and joy through His beloved Son, the Master, has given him positive, true, and eternal joy.

This happiness cannot be taken away. No power on this earth is strong enough to touch it or lessen it. It is an incalculable treasure of which nothing can rob the disciple. It is his for life, and after life, and under all circumstances. He can never again be unhappy after he has once fully participated in this never-ending, life-giving music of the spheres. This is so because the Word is an inexhaustible ocean of bliss, boundless love, and infinite peace. If even a drop of that true happiness be experienced, the pleasures of worldly objects will seem of no worth whatsoever.

Nor is the man or woman who hears this eternal music ever again alone or lonely. Wherever he may wander, the Supreme Creator will always be with him, ever uplifting his heart and soul with the other-worldly strains of the Divine Melody. In the truest sense, he will at all times enjoy the inestimable boon of the companionship of God Himself.

Without coming into conscious contact with the Sound Current, there is no possiblity of real and continuous spiritual progress or abiding happiness. But when it is heard and daily listened to, it will take the disciple across the ocean of mind and matter to the spiritual realms, where all is love and bliss beyond the limited powers of mortal man even to imagine.

The Pearl of Great Price

Man, it must always be remembered, is but a temporary sojourner on this small planet called earth. But once the Master has given him the pearl of great price, the Word, his eyes are opened. He then begins to see that this world is not his home, and that here he is in reality no more than a prodigal son, a feeder of swine among strangers, while far above the light ever burns for him in his Father's palace. He knows then that this world is no more than a dark wilderness as compared with the true home.

> 'This world, which is a wilderness, has been mistaken for a residence.'
>
> *Soami Ji of Agra*

Sitting at the feet of the Master, he is reminded over and over again that above and beyond the narrow confines of this tiny speck of cosmic dust there are innumerable worlds of unimaginable light and beauty, peopled by countless multitudes of supremely happy souls. In gentle, heart-felt words the Master tells him that he may explore these worlds at will, and in this very lifetime.

To the mass of mankind, the gateway to this vast universe of higher worlds is locked and impenetrable, for they wish to hear nothing of it. But for those who are ready for the path, the gate is automatically opened. For the Master holds the key which is the Word—the link between man and his Creator—and he offers it to all who qualify. By rightly using the key, the mortal man can unlock the gate and enter the path that leads ever upward, through all the universe of higher, finer worlds, to the regions of immortality. Then, indeed, does he experience the greatest good fortune that can come to any man.

Says the *Adi Granth*:

> 'Without Shabd (the Word) is darkness within man. In the hands of Sat Guru is the Key, and none else can open the door; and by the highest good fortune alone is the Guru found.'

Jesus, in talking to his disciples prior to their Initiation and being filled with the Holy Ghost, spoke in the same vein, saying:

> 'And I will give unto thee the keys of the kingdom of heaven.'
>
> *Matthew 16 : 19*

When the Master has given the keys of the kingdom to a disciple and the latter proceeds with his spiritual practice, sooner or later the divine music of the Word becomes so enrapturing that all things of the material world are relegated to a minor place. Thereafter the heavenly melody and power draw him upwards with such force that the entire physical world becomes unreal and uninteresting. By the power of the Sound Current, which is with God, and is God, the soul is literally pulled upwards towards the higher realms from which the 'unstruck music' has descended. And in this way the Master and the Word deliver the soul from the material world and the fetters of the mind and senses.

CHAPTER 16

DELIVER US FROM EVIL

'But deliver us from evil.'

—Matthew 6 : 13

In the light of the facts that have been discussed up to this point, it is now possible to indicate the Master's explanation of why so called evil exists in this world.

This, of course, is a question that has vexed men's minds since the beginning of time. For in all ages men have asked: if God really loves us, how can He possibly subject us to the evils of this world and the suffering that we experience here?

And today particularly, because we live in a violent century that has witnessed all manner of evil, hate, suffering, and destruction, there is a stronger tendency than ever to wonder if God has forgotten us or if He really loves us.

To the problem of evil the spiritual science of the Masters offers a solution that explains how and why such conditions can and do exist in the material world, even though that world and all the rest of the universe is ruled by a Supreme Father of infinite love and mercy. In addition, this science shows us clearly and precisely what we should do in order to be delivered from evil.

The key to the solution lies in the fact that this world—the entire physical universe—was created and is now directly governed, not by the Supreme Lord of all creation, but by a subordinate ruler who is himself imperfect, as compared with the purity and perfection of the Supreme Father. This is the ruler who has been referred to as Kal, the negative power, universal mind, and the lord of karma.

This fact, which is entirely new to most people in the western world, must be thoroughly grasped and assimilated. Kal, the negative power, created and now rules over a relatively imperfect world, which was never intended to be a place of unalloyed human happiness. This condition exists, however, by the Will of the all-wise and beneficent Supreme Creator. It appears to be necessary, moreover, because human beings have fallen so far below their original state of absolute purity and perfection.

We are imperfect, even the best of us; far more imperfect than we can realise, as compared with our original state of high and pure spirituality. And this is so because for countless ages we have followed our own desires or, more accurately, the desires of the downward-tending mind. We may deny our imperfection, as many will. But with our microscopic intellect and knowledge, our denials will have but little meaning.

What is high and wonderful to us, for example, may well be low and of little genuine value to the millions of exalted beings who live in higher states.

Next it must be realised that the process by which we became imperfect extended over a period of many millions of years. Our descent from pure spirituality was a slow one, and during it each downward step was the result of our own actions. Now we must retrace our steps.

The only way by which an adequate picture of our present situation can be given to those who are unfamiliar with it is to describe briefly what happened to the prodigal wanderers from Sat Desh, after they first arrived in the material world.

The Four Cycles of Time

The Masters teach that there are four cycles of time, or four ages, that follow each other in this world in the same order again and again, during the periods between dissolutions of

YOGA AND THE BIBLE

146

Age, the Copper Age, and the Iron Age. Of these, the Golden
Age is by far the best, and each of the succeeding ages is
progressively inferior. Each age lasts for many millions of
years, the Golden Age being the longest, and each of the
following ages shorter than the one before.

When those who had descended from Sat Desh first arrived
in the material world they retained somewhat of their original
spirituality. As compared with the mass of mankind today,
for example, their spirituality was of an extermely high
order. Because of this there was at first a Golden Age, and
during it men walked the earth as veritable children of God.
What we today call evil and sin were virtually unknown, for
there could be no evil in the world until mankind's spirituality
had greatly dimished after the passage of an immensely long
period of time.

Gradually, as millions of years passed by, man's spirituality
did slowly diminish. This was due to the soul's association
with the pleasure-loving mind and the senses, and the
consequent indulgence in sense pleasures and the five evil
passions. In one life after another men, using their freedom
to pursue whatever they believed would bring them happiness,
denied their essential spirituality and more and more often
acted selfishly and sensually. As the theologians would say,
they sinned. They thereby sowed the seeds which in subsequent
lives matured as hardships, afflictions, sickness, sorrow,
humiliation, and other happenings that men term evil. We
who are on earth today sowed the wind in ages long past, and
now we are reaping the whirlwind.

But the way to freedom from this world has always been
available to mankind, for one or more of the Masters has
always been present on earth, and could be found by those
who earnestly sought him. It is part of the Creator's design
to send Masters here in all ages, so that they may make those

who long for the return to their true home ready for the upward journey.

The Creator did not make us in the form of puppets. He made us souls that had the right to explore and experience everything that we wished to. But the long and gradual process of degeneration in the material world is an ordained part of the order of Nature that obtains here. Whoever descends as low as this world automatically becomes subject to it. The various Ages must come and go, as they were ordained to from the beginning by the Creator. And the experience of degradation is, apparently, a necessary prerequisite to the process of spiritual regeneration that follows it. It would seem that man must learn by hard-won experience, or he will not learn at all.

The Negative Power

During all of his many lives on earth man has, of course, been in a region that is directly ruled by Kal, the negative power. But Kal, as has been said, rules in strict accordance with the almighty will of the Supreme Creator.

While we are in the realms of the negative power, we are subject to his laws. These are the so-called laws of Nature, and the complex laws of human nature. At the same time, of course, all men are subject to the law of karma, which Kal administers with scrupulous justice and exactitude.

As the negative power, Kal has certain negative qualities, as compared with the supreme purity and perfection of the Supreme Lord, the positive power. When compared with human beings, however, he is a mighty and exalted being, resplendent with light, love, goodness, wisdom, and power. To us, he is a being of unimaginable majesty and grandeur. But in the great universe of universes, Kal is a humble subordinate with delegated and strictly limited powers, which were bestowed on him by the true Lord God, the Supreme Creator of all.

Kal's duties, acting always in accordance with the Supreme Father's Will, are to administer the affairs of the three lower regions—the realm of universal mind, the astral plane, and the physical universe; and to keep individuals and their God-like souls in the material world until their experiences here have purified them to such an extent that they long for release and are ready to start the journey back to their true home. And many of these purifying experiences are of the kind that human beings classify as painful and evil.

To carry out his duties, Kal uses the pleasure—loving mind, the senses, and the five evil passions—lust, anger, greed, attachment, and vanity. The mind, in particular, is a very powerful instrument. The Masters say that it is actually the negative power on a small scale, or that it is the negative power's agent.

Continually deluding and tempting us, these agents of the negative power drive us into seeking happiness in the sense pleasures, the gratification of worldly desires, or the attainment of worldly ambitions. As a result, most people are almost entirely engrossed in the pursuit of worldly enjoyments or material goals, and these cause them to forget the existence of the soul and the need for spiritual aspiration and effort.

But the negative power is imperfect and, as a consequence, his worldly pleasures are likewise imperfect. They do not give lasting satisfaction and many of them create reactions of guilt, remorse, jealousy, sorrow, unhappiness, and even bleak despair and utter woe. These are among the things that we call painful and evil, and often blame upon an unjust God, even though they may be the result of our own past actions. Their ultimate purpose, as has been pointed out, is to cause human beings to grow weary of this world and to long for a higher and more perfect way of life.

Actually, it is usually as the result of bitter experience alone that men can be made to open their eyes and seek for the path of love and light. The sooner this is brought about the better; of that there is no doubt. And so it often happens that the more acutely men experience the evil known as suffering, the better it is for them. Suffering then is a great blessing in disguise.

In addition to his other duties, Kal, as has been said, is also the lord of karma, and administers the operation of the karmic law. It is his duty, therefore, to see to it that everything we do unto others is in due course of time done unto us. As a consequence, much that is classed as evil comes into peoples lives—illness, apparent injustice, false friends, poverty, and hardships of all kinds.

If we but knew it, these are not injustices or evils thrust upon us by an unknown God or the 'hand of fate'. They are injustices and evils that we ourselves have at one time or another thrust upon others. The Supreme Father does not arbitrarily send into our lives tragedy, sickness, or any other painful or 'evil' experience. We bring these things into our lives through our own karmas.

The material world, as has been pointed out, is primarily a training school, and so-called evil is one of the absolutely necessary taskmasters. Without it we would never learn and would never begin the search for the Way back to our Father's house. It can readily be understood that if there were only happiness in this world, people would be contented with it and would make no efforts to discover the higher worlds. And, in accordance with the laws established by the Creator, individual effort is essential. We are not intended, it has been said, to become machine-made angels without the expenditure of any effort of our own.

The laws administered by the negative power, together with our own misdoings, produce results that seem painful and evil to us, of that there is no doubt. But in the long run they are utterly beneficial since they lead to our greatest possible good—spiritual growth, escape from this dark and low world, and ultimate return to our homeland in Sat Desh.

But even while living in the dominions of Kal, man, according to the plan of the Creator, is intended to experience much happiness and relatively little pain. The intent of the plan, the Masters teach, is to give man just as much happiness as possible consistent with the ultimate purpose of guiding him back to the spiritual realms. The entire plan was designed by our Creator for our benefit, and those who meet their difficulties in the right spirit will profit by them.

There are many, no doubt who will ask why the process of human decline and subsequent redemption must be such a long and painful one. Why, since the Creator is all-powerful, does He not purify souls in an instant, instead of permitting them to wander for so many ages in the dark material worlds?

The Masters teach that the Supreme Father's method is the best, the most loving, and in fact, the only right way in accordance with the laws of life established by the Creator to enable us to regain our original spirituality.

In accordance with these laws, the only right method is to allow those of lower spirituality to live in a region in which they can have choice of action. In that way, and that way alone, will they learn by needed experience, and learn the needed lessons completely and for all time.

Spiritual regeneration, the Masters teach, should not be brought about in the twinkling of an eye by giving higher spirituality—to say nothing of the radiantly pure spirituality of Sat Desh—to an individual of lower spirituality. This would only be a source of misery. The receiver, far from welcoming his higher state would dislike it because he would not yet be ready for it. Using a homely simile, the Masters say that if a cow were to be suddenly given the spirituality of a human being, the result could only be misery for the cow.

To accord with the Creator's laws, the ground must first be prepared by the individual's own efforts. And this preparation and these efforts are brought about in the best and only right way as a result of the individual's experiences in the realms of the negative power, where he can act precisely as he pleases—and then observe the results of his actions.

How so-called evil originated in this world, and the purpose of its existence may now perhaps be better understood. It was designed by the Supreme Father for our benefit as part of His divine plan, and as the only right and practicable experience in accordance with immutable laws that could purify us and make us ready for our homeward journey. The reason for evil and our struggle against it is to cleanse our enemy, the pleasure-loving mind, and inspire in us a longing to rise above the low material world and seek the path that leads us to our true and ultimate destiny.

There is much more than a modicum of truth in the apostle Paul's saying that:

'Whom the Lord loveth, he chasteneth.'
Hebrews 12 : 6

The Masters, from their infinitely higher standpoint, see in evil only a state of incompleteness, a phase of growth, and a necessary spur to individual evolution. But the average human being has a more limited viewpoint. He cannot see the overall plan and the role of teacher that so-called evil plays in that plan. To him, as a rule, evil is anything that he does not like. Thus, a thoroughly immoral person likes and enjoys immorality—until it begins to pall and to sicken his or her soul. But a person who, by the aid of his karmic experiences, has evolved to the stage where he has finished with immorality dislikes it and regards it as an evil thing.

And so the Supreme Father, planning throughout eternity for the redemption and purification of His children, regards discipline for evil-doing as a relative or lesser good which, once the lesson has been thoroughly learnt, will teach the evil-doer to search for the spiritual path.

This is the destiny of all true spiritual seekers. If one misses this divine experience in the present lifetime, the Supreme One will still look after him with infinite love and mercy. But He is in no hurry and gives His children a free rein. The purifying process may take many lifetimes. Still, in due time each one will be cleansed and brought to the point where he will gladly and with great rejoicing fulfil the Father's purpose.

From the exalted viewpoint of the Supreme One, there is no such thing as evil. For he knows what is genuinely best for all, and His divine plan works unceasingly for the highest happiness of all, through their gradual redemption and salvation.

In view of all these facts it can be seen that everything which men call evil in this world, involving suffering of any sort, has as its ultimate objective to bring the sufferer to the path of love and spirituality. That means the path of the Masters. For the Masters alone, together with the power of the divine Word, can finally and irrevocably deliver us from evil and from the rulership of the negative power. At the time of initiation the Masters take over responsibility for our lives and our karma, and from that time onward we are under their protection and guarded against the devices of the negative power and so-called evil.

Despite the fact that we are immediately under the rule of the negative power, it is also true that the Supreme Father is in this world and is in us. It is He, and not the negative power, who is basically guiding our destiny; and he uses the negative power simply as a necessary instrument to bring His prodigal children back to their heavenly home.

Sooner or later, the true seekers will reach the point at which the meeting with a living perfect Master, and ensuing deliverance from evil, is assured. This is as certain as that the sun will rise tomorrow morning.

It is only a question of time, experience, and the working out of karma.

CHAPTER 17

FROM DEATH UNTO LIFE

'He that heareth my word (the Word)...is passed from death unto life.'

—*John 5 : 24*

'I die daily.'

—*1 Corinthians 15 : 31*

This statement made by St Paul has usually been interpreted to mean that if we would hear and heed his teachings as given in the New Testament, we would enter after death into a higher and possibly an eternal life.

But the far more probable meaning is that those whom Jesus connected with the Sound Current of the Word would be passed from the relative death of living in the body to the experience of the finer and much more real life of one of the higher or heavenly worlds. This, of course, is what always happens to the disciples of a living Master after they have advanced some little distance on the path.

To Jesus, as to other Masters, the radiant life of the kingdom of heaven was by no means a far-off thing, to be realised only after death. To the contrary, it was a very present reality, to be entered upon here and now. All of the great Masters have taught this identical truth, and have shown their disciples how to enter and visit the worlds of higher life while still living on earth in the body.

When Jesus spoke of this fact, his message was not understood. And this has always been the case. Even today, among people assumed to be much more enlightened than those of two thousand years ago, there are but few who can realise that this is the truth. They have been taught about a heaven to which they may go after death, and that seems quite possibly true. But when they are told that they can enter the higher kingdoms now, while in the body and in full consciousness, they tend to regard the idea as impossible, if not preposterous.

Yet passing in full consciousness from the death of this low world to the abounding life of one of the higher kingdoms of the Father was one of the major points of Jesus' message, as it has always been a cardinal point in the message of all genuine Masters who teach the true meaning of the Word of God. With these Masters and their disciples it is no half-understood theory or doctrine, but a vital and life-giving daily experience.

Another fact should now be understood. It is that the experience of entering the higher worlds while still living, as taught by the Masters of the Word, is identical with that which takes place at the time of death. The only difference is that the disciples of the Master carry out the experience voluntarily, while the process of death is involuntary. Death comes at the time preordained for it by the individual's karma, and, in actuality, the continuity of life is no more broken when the breath leaves the body than is the continuity of child life broken by the incident of birth. So-called death is the means by which the life of humans is liberated, becoming more intense, more real.

When one understands this, he knows what the apostle Paul meant when he said: 'I die daily.' Doing precisely as present-day disciples do, he stilled his mind during his daily meditation and left the body to rise into the fairer and finer worlds of the Father's kingdom.

When the disciple pierces the veil, passes through the 'tenth door', which in reality is 'not thicker than the wing of a butterfly', and goes inside and up to higher worlds, the body remains in the position in which he left it. The life processes slow down almost to a standstill, but the body remains in perfect health until its owner is ready to return to it. He may remain out of the body for hours, or even days, but at any moment can return to it at will and resume his daily life on earth.

During this time the disciple is never asleep or unconscious—not for a single moment. In fact, the reverse is true. For the first time, he begins not only to believe in the heavenly kingdoms but to visit them and know them; and the new existence that he knows and takes part in is filled with life and light and joy. He sees life from a higher vantage ground, with renewed vision, new hopes, and moving in loftier spheres of thought and experience. When this experience has been achieved, all the riches, fortunes, and pleasures of the material world become insignificant in comparison. Having passed through the gates of death, the disciple has become heir to immortality.

Death is mankind's last enemy, and the power of God incarnate in and flowing through the Master grants victory over death by initiation into the process of withdrawing the soul from the body while one is still living.

The soul, as it rises above the body consciousness in this experience, shines forth in all its pristine purity and comes into cosmic awareness. In the Indian scriptures this elevation of the soul is called 'Duaya Janma' or the second birth, that is, the birth of the spirit as distinct from the birth of the flesh.

In the higher world which the disciple first enters, and where he sees many who have reached great heights of spiritual power and purity, he feels his own being expand with an infinite longing for growth and always more growth in the knowledge of God and His ways. For him now, nothing else matters. All else is superficial, and the earth is seen to be merely a training school for the soul. Only the presence and power and life and bliss of God and living in His pesence are seen to be real and enduring, and in them are all joy and perfection and satisfaction.

The disciple now has discovered a brighter and more radiant world, where never the sun sets, never clouds lower, never hearts are broken; a world where always the inhabitants desire God's will above all else and where His Holy Will is seen to be the acme and essence of all that is good and true and beautiful. In this higher world is beauty beyond earth words to describe or earth minds to conceive. There is radiance of colour and light which the earth-bound artist has never achieved, and an all-embracing atmosphere of joy and gladness, worship, and love and vibrant life that puts earth life to shame.

> 'Eye hath not seen nor ear heard neither have entered into the heart of man the things which God hath prepared for them that love him.'
>
> *I Corinthians 2 : 9*

When a disciple passes from death into life and enters one of the higher worlds, he sees that everything that is considered beautiful on earth is but a faint and imperfect reflection of the higher and more beautiful things that fill the heavenly kingdoms. It is this that Plato meant when he said that the physical world is a faint reflection of the world of Ideas (the astral world). The disciple, on entering the higher worlds, sees and knows the truth about the physical world and the brighter, higher worlds that Shelley spoke of when pondering the death of his friend:

> 'Peace, peace! He is not dead, he doth not sleep
> He hath awakened from the dream of life.
> 'Tis we who, lost in stormy visions, keep
> With phantoms an unprofitable strife.
> He has outsoared the shadow of our night.'

The daily experience of passing from death into life brings to a complete end any and all fear of death. For the Master and his disciples know what comes after death, as well as they know any ordinary fact of this life. They have learnt how to pass at will through the gates of death, to see what is there, and then return to their ordinary earth life, at any time and as often as they wish.

The procedure of 'dying daily' and so passing from death unto life has always been a familiar one to the great spiritual Masters of the east. This is clearly shown by their many statements concerning it. The following are but a few out of many examples.

Maulana Rum, the great Persian Master, wrote:

'Rise thou, O soul, and come thou up before thy death; and behold thou thy kingdom and thy eternal Home.'
'If life dost thou desire, then before thy death do thou die, O friend.'
'Of dying before death the secret is this, that after such a dying divine blessings dost thou receive.'
'Thou art such that besides this (physical) body thou hast another (astral) body. Do not therefore be afraid of getting out of the mortal frame.'

Guru Nanak many times expressed the same truths :

'Such a spiritual practice do thou follow, O Nanak, that diest thou even while living.'
'Go while alive to the place where you are to go after death.'
'Seeing without (physical) eyes, hearing without ears, walking without feet, working without hands, speaking without tongue, thus dying while living: In this way, O Nanak, do thou reach the Lord by knowing His Will.'

Kabir Sahib put the same thought in the words:

'Death, of which the people are so very much afraid, is a source of peace and joy to me.'

Dadu Sahib, another great Saint, exclaims:

> 'O Dadu! Learn to die while alive, for in the end all must die.'

Bulleh Shah wrote:

> 'If before thy death dost thou die, this dying shall bear (divine) fruit.'
> In the Holy Koran the prophet Mohammed says:

> *'Before thy death do thou die.'*

'Whoever dieth before his death, getteth he relieved of a world of sorrow; whoever flieth out of the (material) universe, getteth he delivered from the universe.'

These quotations have been given at some length because they show so clearly that the procedure of 'going within' and 'dying daily' in order to enter the kingdom of heaven and experience the fruits of the spiritual birth has been known and taught, not only by Jesus and the apostle Paul, but by all the great Masters of the east as well. This is a fact that is not yet widely realised in the western countries, though it has been known for centuries by many in the east.

Words of opposition are powerless to shake the faith of a disciple when he has once had this experience, for he has seen with his own inner eye, and knows that the teaching of the Masters is true. Death has become voluntary and he knows that the radiant life beyond the veil is a fact. The material world appears as a dream to him; but under instructions from his Master he returns to it and carries on with his mundane existence. But material things have lost their fascination for him, and the material world no longer possesses the power to interest him completely, as it did before.

For the process of dying daily and thus passing from death unto life as taught by the perfect Masters, brings a joy passing all understanding of those still bound and confined by physical matter.

CHAPTER 18

THE LIFE EVERLASTING

'He that heareth my word (the Word)...hath everlasting life.'

—John 5 : 24

'And this is life eternal, that they might know thee, the only true God.'

—John 17 : 3

It can now be realised that the spiritual science of the Masters is not an orthodox religion, a system of ceremonial rites, or a code of creeds or dogmas. It is an entirely spiritual and scientifically demonstrable method of finding and following to the end the path that leads to the true God and the true heavenly home of everlasting life. Many, with the aid of a living Master, have already reached the homeland by following this self-same path. Others, who wish to follow it with sufficient earnestness, will surely find the way.

The path of the Masters is not an imaginative or symbolical term. It is a definite road that the disciple travels in the company of his Master, who has many times journeyed the full length of the way. This path leads the traveller from earth higher and higher through one heavenly kingdom after another, each one more radiant with beauty and splendour, until the Master brings the disciple at last to Sat Desh, the region of everlasting spiritual life.

Life in these higher worlds, the realms of the everlasting life, though indescribable in earth language, is infinitely and immeasurably superior to life here on earth. Actually, no comparison is possible, for in their spirit substance and arrangement these worlds are wholly unlike anything known here.

Of certain facts, however, related by the Masters who call those worlds their home, the reader may have no doubts. No one who has risen to take part in the eternal life of Sat Desh has ever had any regrets over leaving behind him the far lower and more limited life here on earth. For no one in Sat Desh is ever unhappy, or ever suffers from any conceivable kind of ill or imperfection. For them there is no sorrow and no death. Life in our true home, in short, is a perfect one in every way, and the countless multitudes of pure souls that live there may be described in earth terms as being radiantly and blissfully happy.

What more can be said? All of the great Masters of the Word have said that life in Sat Desh is perfection. And perfection means that there cannot be anything better.

The Beginning of the Upward Journey

When the disciple is initiated, he reaches the starting point of his actual homeward journey. With the ever-present help of the Master, he will now break every fetter that binds him to the lower worlds and, borne upward on the wings of the divine power that is the Word, will reach the regions of eternal life.

This journey is started while the disciple is living on earth in the physical body. For, as has many times been pointed out, we are not confined to the physical body even while still living in it. We are imprisoned in the body only because we do not know how to get out of it. How to leave the body at will and enter the higher regions is one of the first lessons which the Masters teach to their disciples.

Essentially, the method commences with the daily practice of meditation in which the attention is concentrated and centred at the third eye—the gateway to the higher worlds. Sooner or later, according to the rate of progress made, the disciple's astral body, together with the causal body, the mind and the soul, will pass out through the 'third eye' in the forehead and will enter the astral region. This is situated just beyond the topmost border of the physical universe. It is in the region of 'And', the second grand division.

The disciple 'is now in the position of a man who has been all of his life confined in a semi-dark prison and has just been given his freedom,' says Dr Julian P. Johnson in his book, *With a Great Master in India*. 'He steps out from behind prison walls into a beautiful park or garden in front of the prison, ready to begin his journey home. In fact, he is now ready to actually begin to live, his freedom is intoxicating, joyous.

'At this point the student traveller enjoys so many new sensations that he is quite bewildered. He is fairly intoxicated with delight. He is conscious of a marvellous influx of power. His vision is lucid. Space is obliterated. Time has disappeared; for now all events stand before him clearly outlined, the past, the present, and the future.

'He now realises the shadowy nature of the lower world from which he has just escaped. He beholds its pitiful limitations, its passing deceptive show, its panorama of births and deaths, under the wheel of karma, or the law of cause and effect. All of these things are now clear to his illuminated consciousness, and yet he has taken but the first step on the path of the Masters. For the royal highway begins just as you step through the tenth door, out of the physical body, and into the first astral zone.'

'This is the true interpretation of Plato's famous 'myth of the cave .'

It is here that the disciple first meets his Master in his radiant form. From that moment on, the radiant form is his constant companion, and leads the way on the upward journey.

The disciple is now in a world he never saw before and of the very existence of which most people are unaware. But it is a world which impresses itself upon the traveller as being much more real than this world. It is also much finer and more beautiful, and full of light and joy.

Here there is a great variety of scenery of awe-inspiring beauty, landscapes, rivers, and mountains, meadows, forests, and buildings. Also there are multitudes of people, gathered from every nation and tribe on earth. The disciple converses with them, for there all languages are understood by all. The light and colours of this world surpass anything on this poor earth, beautiful though it may have seemed before. All of these things the disciple looks upon for the first time, and with a new eye which he never consciously used before. He is now functioning in his astral body and using his astral senses for communication, just as he used his physical senses before.

Guided by the Master in his radiant form the disciple now enters the Capital, the indescribably beautiful, Sahansdal Kanwal, meaning the 'Thousand Petalled Lotus', a marvellous region of light and beauty, indescribable in human language. Here there are one thousand and one glowing lights—one large centre light surrounded by a thousand smaller ones. Each light is of a different tint or colour, and all are clustered together somewhat in the form of an immense celestial lotus flower.

This radiant group of brilliant but softly glowing lights is sometimes called Koh-i-Noor, or the 'Mountain of Light'. It is in fact the power house of the physical universe. From it, as from a giant dynamo, goes forth the power that creates, sustains, and controls the entire creation below the astral world, all the millions of suns, stars, and galaxies, each moving in its appointed orbit, that make up the incredible vastness of the physical universe.

In the astral region, says Guru Nanak:

'Day and night shineth the pure Flame, and Guru's devotee knoweth this inner lamp...By the grace of Guru is the Flame manifested.'

Paltu Sahib, in speaking of this light, says:

'In the heavens is an inverted well, and in it burneth a lamp. In it the lamp burneth without oil and without wick, and keepeth it burning day and night for all the six seasons and the twelve months. He who hath found Sat Guru beholdeth that Light; for those who have not Sat Guru invisible doth it remain.'

The Journey Continues

The disciple may spend some months or even years in visiting the astral worlds before he advances to the next higher region. The length of time depends upon his karma, the difficulties he meets within himself, and the general fitness with which he entered upon the path. Eventually, however, the Master will take him to the second region on the path, the realm of universal mind, and in it the disciple functions in his mental or causal body.

Much of what is there cannot be told in human language, for there is nothing on earth with which it can be compared. It can only be said that as the disciple goes continually higher on the path, he begins to see with an ever clearer eye the wonder and the glory of God's purposes. With each upward step the majesty of the Creator's work stands forth in vaster and more overpowering splendour.

When the disciple reaches this region, he finds himself in possession of new powers and understanding never before realised. In fact, he has to grow as he advances. That is one reason why it often takes a considerable period of time to reach the higher regions. One must be gradually fitted for their higher and purer spiritual atmosphere.

It is in the causal world, the home of universal mind, that the self or soul of the disciple discards its mind, no longer needing it for contact or communication with the surrounding world. The soul or spirit alone, free of the material, astral, and causal bodies, goes on and up into the next region, the third stage on the path of the Masters.

When the disciple reaches the third region, he once more gains a vast increase of spiritual power and understanding. But there is a constantly increasing difficulty as one rises higher in describing anything that is seen or heard in the higher regions. They are so far removed, and so different from the earth. The very ideas in the higher regions are beyond the grasp of earth's inhabitants and cannot be described in earthly language.

The attainment of the third region marks an important stage of advancement in the upward progress of the soul. Here it leaves behind the last remnants of earthly impurities and, wholly purified, functions without any covering or body of any kind. Here, for the first time, it is able to see itself as it really is, and always has been, pure spirit, a child of the Supreme Lord, a drop of the ocean. Here for the first time it is absolutely untrammelled and gloriously free. And from this region it returns no more to be born on earth.

From this time on all of the soul's tendencies are upwards. The attraction of the still higher regions and the soul's longing to reach its source becomes overwhelming, and it is impatient to go on. Being now free of all impurities, the soul here attains a brilliancy equal to twelve of our suns, and now it rises rapidly to the still more perfect regions above.

The lord or ruler of the fourth region is known as Sohang, and the meaning of his name is , 'What thou art, the same am

I'. When the disciple reaches the fourth region and beholds the majestic and awe-inspiring beauty and grandeur of its lord, the realisation comes to him with overwhelming joy: 'I am That! That am I!' At that moment of sublime realisation, the disciple knows, and knows for ever, that he is one with the Supreme One.

Says Guru Nanak:

> 'By Sohang know thou thyself through the secret of the Word.'

The fourth region is the gateway to the mansion of the lord of the fifth region, which is called Sach Khand, the True or Imperishable Region. This region is in the lower part of Sat Desh, the vast and indescribably beautiful highest spiritual realm, the real or abiding country. Its lord, who is Sat Purush (true Lord or God), is the great Father and the Lord of us all and of all regions below Him. He is boundless love and light, wisdom, intelligence, and power. His kingdom is the lost world of beauty, light, peace, and joy that all men seek, and on this earth can never find.

The disciple has now reached the region of immortality and of truth. He has known the truth, through the grace of his Master, and it has indeed set him free. While still in the lower regions of Brahmand, he is always liable to return to earth, and to rebirth and death. But when he reaches the purely spiritual region of Sat Desh, the first plane of which is the fifth region on the path of the Masters, there is no more return to earth, except he be sent there as a redeemer. For Sat Desh is the region of the eternal, everlasting life.

Here the disciple enters upon the full reward of his long course of training and devotion to the Master. He becomes a Saint himself; and the mission of his Master is finished, so far as this journey is concerned. The Master has brought him to his true home, fulfilling the promise:

'I am the Way, the Truth, and the Life.'

John 14 : 6

The Higher Regions

But the soul has yet to travel over the most sublime and beautiful part of its journey. Above the fifth region, as has been pointed out, there are three other heavenly regions, all of utterly inconceivable splendour. But from here on the great ruler of the fifth region takes over the responsibility of guiding the soul to the end of its journey. By his great love and light, he directs the soul through all of the remaining regions. First the soul becomes united with the very essence of the lord of the fifth region, and so partakes of all his attributes. He then advances to the three remaining regions.

Finally, at the ultimate end of its journey, the soul arrives at Radha Soami Dham, the mansion of the Supreme Lord God, the region of the Nameless One who, though no name can describe Him, is called Radha Soami the Lord of the soul. He is the Supreme Lord of all that exists.

No human thought can embrace the glory of the Supreme Lord God; no earthly language can tell of Him. He is the formless, all-embracing, omnipresent One. He is the impersonal, infinite ocean of love in which, in reality, we all abide. From Him flows all life and spirituality, all truth, all love, and all reality. He is all wisdom, love, and power. All of the lords of all regions are His manifestations. He taking form, and many forms, in order that His beneficent purposes may be carried out in all the infinite creation. They are all His forms; but none of them expresses His totality. He may take millions of forms but He himself remains formless, impersonal, all-pervading. He is universal spirit, universal life; the spiritual essence of all that is. His heavenly kingdom is the infinite and eternal ocean of reality and spirituality.

Of the highest of all regions, Soami Ji of Agra says:

'The soul has now seen the three regions above Sach Khand (the True Region) and the ruling lord in each one. He has seen them and united his own being with them. All he can say is that here in these holy Regions, love plays the supreme part. It is all love.'

The soul has now reached the end of the path of the saints. It has been led stage by stage, from the low levels of this dark planet earth to the highest realms of spirituality, purity, and bliss. During the course of the journey the disciple has changed from a circumscribed, limited human being, driven by the base desires of the mind and the five earthly passions, to a god of unimaginable glory, wisdom and power.

Through the help of the Master and the spiritual power of the Word he has put off this mortal flesh and become immortal. He now knows and is one with the true God, and through merging himself into Him has become a sharer in the life eternal of the highest realms. What he has now become must for ever remain beyond the powers of understanding of the ordinary earth dweller.

Looking back to his cramped and crawling life on earth, he may sometimes remember when he first met his Master, gazed into his serene and radiant eyes glowing with spirituality and overflowing with love and compassion for all mankind, and listened as he said:

'Come let us return to our own Home. Why live in a foreign land?'

The position and the mission of the Master, or Saint, must now be apparent. The journey of salvation, the safe return to the higher regions, can never be made without him, either in this life or after human death. Therefore the perfect Master is the supreme necessity, if one is to reach those regions. For this reason, the way to those regions is called the path of the Saints. Happy indeed is the soul who takes shelter with a Saint and undertakes a journey in company with him. Among all the children of men, he is the most supremely fortunate.

Such souls, say the Masters, dwell in everlasting bliss.

ADDRESSES FOR INFORMATION AND BOOKS

INDIAN SUB-CONTINENT

INDIA
The Secretary
Radha Soami Satsang Beas
P.O. Dera Baba Jaimal Singh 143204
District Amritsar, Punjab

NEPAL
Mr. Dal Bahadur Shreshta
Radha Soami Satsang Beas
P. O. Box 1646, Gongabu, Dhapasi
Kathmandu
☎+97-1-435-7765

PAKISTAN
Mr. Sadrang Seetal Das
Lahori Mohala
Larkana, Sindh

SRI LANKA
Mr. Chandroo Mirpuri
39/3 Horton Place
Colombo 7

SOUTHEAST ASIA

FOR FAR EAST
Mrs. Cami Moss
RSSB-HK
T.S.T., P.O. Box 90745
Kowloon, Hong Kong
☎+852-2369-0625

MALAYSIA
Mr. Selvarajoo Pragasam
No. 15 Jalan SL 10/4
Bandar Sungai Long, Selangor
43000 Kajang

THAILAND
Mr. Harmahinder Singh Sethi
58/32 Rachdapitsek Road, Soi 16
Thapra, Bangkok Yai
Bangkok 10600
☎+66-2-868-2186 / 2187

INDONESIA
Mr. Ramesh Sadarangani
Jalan Pasir Putih IV/16, Block E 4
Ancol Timur, Jakarta
DKI Jakarta 14430

PHILIPPINES
Mr. Kay Sham
Science of the Soul Study Center
9001 Don Jesus Boulevard
Alabang Hills, Cupang 1771
Muntinlupa City, Metro Manila
☎+63-2-772-0111 / 0555

SINGAPORE
Mrs. Asha Melwani
Radha Soami Satsang Beas Singapore
19 Amber Road, Singapore 439868
☎+65-6447-4956

ASIA PACIFIC

AUSTRALIA
Mr. Pradeep Raniga
P.O. Box 642
Balwyn North, Victoria 3104

NEW ZEALAND
Mr. Tony Waddicor
Science of the Soul Study Centre
P. O. Box 5331, Auckland
☎+64-9-624-2202

GUAM
Mrs. Hoori M. Sadhwani
115 Alupang Cove
241 Condo Lane, Tamuning 96911

HONG KONG
Mr. Manoj Sabnani
RSSB-HK, 3rd Floor, Eader Centre
39-41 Hankow Road,
Tsimshatsui, Kowloon
☎+852-2369-0625

JAPAN
Mr. Jani G. Mohinani
Radha Soami Satsang Beas
1-2-18 Nakajima-Dori
Aotani, Chuo-Ku
Kobe 651-0052
☎+81-78-222-5353

*SOUTH KOREA,
TAIWAN, R.O.C.*
Mr. Haresh Buxani,
3rd floor, Eader Centre
39-41 Hankow Road
Tsimshatsui, Kowloon
Hong Kong

UNITED STATES
Mr. Hank Muller
20038 Indigo Lake Drive
Magnolia, TX 77355

Dr. Vincent P. Savarese
2550 Pequeno Circle
Palm Springs, CA 92264-9522

Dr. Frank E. Vogel
275 Cutts Road
Newport, NH 03773

Dr. Douglas Torr
215 Ridgeview Road
Southern Pines, NC 28387

Science of the Soul Study Center
4115 Gillespie Street
Fayetteville, NC 28306-9053
☎+1-910-426-5306

Science of the Soul Study Center
2415 East Washington Street
Petaluma, CA 94954-9274
☎+1-707-762-5082

NORTH AMERICA

CANADA
Mr. John Abel
#701-1012 Beach Avenue
Vancouver, B.C. V6E 1T7

Mrs. Meena Khanna
149 Elton Park Road
Oakville, Ontario L6J 4C2

MEXICO
Dr. Hector Esponda
Gambao 111-3
Guadalajara, Jalisco 44100

CARIBBEAN

FOR CARIBBEAN
Mr. Sean Finnigan
R.S.S.B. Foundation
P. O. Box 978, Phillipsburg
St. Maarten, N. A.
☎+599-547-0066

BARBADOS, W.I.
Mrs. Jaya Sabnani
1 Sunset Drive South
Fort George Heights
St. Michael BB111 02

CURACAO, N.A.
Mrs. Reshma Jethmalani
Science of the Soul Study Centre
Kaya Seru di Milon 6-9
Santa Catharina
☎+599-9-747-0226

GRENADA, W.I.
Mr. Prakash Amarnani
P.O. Box 726, St. Georges

GUYANA
Mrs. Indu Lalwani
115, Garnette Street,
Newtown Kitty, Georgetown

HAITI, W.I
Mrs. Mousson Finnigan
P.O. Box 2314, Port-au-Prince

JAMAICA, W.I.
Mrs. Reshma Daswani
17 Colombus Height
First Phase, Ocho Rios

ST. MAARTEN, N.A.
Mr. Haresh Balani
R.S.S.B. Foundation
P. O. Box 978, Phillipsburg
☎+599-547-0066

ST. THOMAS
Mrs. Hema Melwani
P.O. Box 600145
USVI-VI00801-6145

SURINAME
Mr. Chandru Samtani
15 Venus Straat, Elizabetshof
Paramaribo

TRINIDAD, W.I.
Mr. Chandru Chatlani
20 Admiral Court
Westmoorings-by-Sea, Westmoorings

CENTRAL AMERICA

BELIZE
Mrs. Milan Bhindu Hotchandani
5789 Philip Goldson Avenue
Kings Park, Belize City

PANAMA
Mr. Ashok Tikamdas Dinani
P.O. Box 0302, 00830 Colon

SOUTH AMERICA

FOR SOUTH AMERICA
Mr. Hiro W. Balani
Edificio Marina, Paseo De Farola, 3-6
Malaga, Spain 29016

ARGENTINA
Mrs. Fabiana Shilton
Super 1 14D8 3°A, Post Code 1426
Buenos Aires

BRAZIL
Mr. Guillerme Almedia
SQN 315, Bloco C
Apto. 306 Brasilia
DF 70-774-030

CHILE
Mr. Vijay Harjani
Pasaje Cuatro No. 3438
Sector Chipana, Iquique

COLOMBIA
Mrs. Emma Orozco
Calle 45, #99-25, Medellin 49744

ECUADOR
Dr. Fernando Flores Villalva
Radha Soami Satsang Beas-Ecuador
Calle Marquez de Varela
OE 3-68y Avda. America
P.O. Box 17-21-115, Quito
☎+5932-2-555-988

PERU
Mr. Carlos Fitts
Av. Rinconada Del, Lago 664
Lima 12

VENEZUELA
Mr. Jose Penaherrera
RSSB-Venezuela, Av. Los Samanes con
Av. Los Naranjos Conj
Res. Florida 335, Caracas 1012

EUROPE

AUSTRIA
Mr. Hansjorg Hammerer
Sezenweingasse 10, A-5020 Salzburg

BELGIUM
Mr. Piet J. E. Vosters
Driezenstraat 26, Turnhout 2300

BULGARIA
Mr. Deyan Stoyanov
Foundation Radha Soami Satsang Beas
P. O. Box 39, 8000 Bourgas

CYPRUS
Mr. Heraclis Achilleos
P. O. Box 29077, 1035 Nicosia

CZECH REPUBLIC
Mr. Vladimir Skalsky
Maratkova 916, 142 00 Praha 411

DENMARK
Mr. Tony Sharma
Sven Dalsgaardsvej 33, DK-7430 Ikast

FINLAND
Ms. Anneli Wingfield
P. O. Box 1422, 00101 Helsinki

FRANCE
Mr. Pierre de Proyart
7 Quai Voltaire, Paris 75007

GERMANY
Mr. Rudolf Walberg
P. O. Box 1544
D-65800 Bad Soden / Taunus

GIBRALTAR
Mr. Sunder Mahtani
RSSB Charitable Trust Gibraltar
15 Rosia Road
☎+350-412-67

GREECE
Mr. Themistoclis Gianopoulos
6 Platonos Str.
17672 Kallithea, Attiki

ITALY
Mrs. Wilma Salvatori Torri
Via Bacchiglione 3, 00199 Rome

*THE NETHERLANDS
(HOLLAND)*
Radha Soami Satsang Beas - Nederland
Middenweg 145 E
1394 AH Nederhorst den Berg
☎+31-294-255-255

Mr. Henk Keuning
Kleizuwe2, Vreeland 3633AE

NORWAY
Mr. Manoj Kaushal
Langretta 8
N-1279 Oslo

POLAND
Mr. Vinod Sharma
ul. 1go Sierpnia 36 B, M-100
PL-02-134 Warsaw

PORTUGAL
Mrs. Sharda Lodhia
Torres das Palmeiras, Lote 68, 11° C
2780-145 Oeiras

ROMANIA
Mrs. Carmen Cismas
C.P. 6-12
810600 Braila

SLOVENIA
Mr. Marko Bedina,
Brezje pri Trzicu 68, 4290 Trzic

SPAIN
Mr. J. W. Balani
Calle Panorama no. 15
Cerrado de Calderon
29018 Malaga

SWEDEN
Mr. Lennart Zachen
Norra Sonnarpsvägen 29
SE-286 72 Asljunga

SWITZERLAND
Mr. Sebastian Züst-
Weissenrainstrasse 48
CH 8707 Uetikon am See

UNITED KINGDOM
Mr. Narinder Singh Johal
Haynes Park, Haynes
MK45 3BL Bedford
☎+44-1234-381-234

AFRICA

BENIN
Mr. Jaikumar T. Vaswani
01 Boite Postale 951,
Recette Principale, Cotonou 01

BOTSWANA
Dr. Krishan Lal Bhateja
P. O. Box 402539
Gaborone

CONGO
Mr. Prahlad Parbhu
143 Kasai Ave. Lubumbashi

GHANA
Mr. Murli Chatani
Radha Soami Satsang Beas
P. O. Box 3976, Accra
☎+233-242-057-309

IVORY COAST
Mr. Konan N'Dri
Boite Postale 569, Abidjan 08

KENYA
Mr. Surinder Singh Ghir
35 Mutty Court
(Kipepu RD), Nairobi

LESOTHO
Mr. Sello Wilson Moseme
P. O. Box 750, Leribe 300

LIBYA (G.S.P.L.A.J.)
Mr. Roshan Lal
P.O. Box 38930, Bani Walid

MADAGASCAR
Mr. Francis Murat
Villa 8-02 Residence D'Ambatobe
Antananarivo 101

MAURITIUS
Dr. I. Fagoonee
17 Manick Avenue
La Louise, Quatre Bornes

NAMIBIA
Mrs. Jennifer Carvill
P. O. Box 449
Swakopmund 9000

NIGERIA
Mr. Nanik N. Balani
G.P.O. Box 5054, Marina
Lagos

RÉUNION
Ms. Marie-Lynn Marcel
5 Chemin 'Gonneau, BernSica,
St Gillesles Hauts 97435

SIERRA LEONE
Mr. Kishore S. Mahboobani
82/88 Kissy Dock Yard,
P O Box 369, Freetown

SOUTH AFRICA
Mr. Gordon Clive Wilson
P. O. Box 47182
Greyville 4023

Radha Soami Satsang Beas – SA
P.O. Box 5270, Cresta 2118
☎+27-11-792-7644

SWAZILAND
Mr. Peter Dunseith
P. O. Box 423, Mbabane

TANZANIA
Mr. D.N. Pandit
P.O. Box 1963
Dar-Es-Salaam

UGANDA
Mr. Sylvester Kakooza
Radha Soami Satsang Beas
P. O. Box 31381, Kampala

ZAMBIA
Mr. Chrispin Lwali
P.O. Box 12094, Chingola

ZIMBABWE
Mr. G.D. Wright
Pharmanova
P. O. Box 1726, Harare

MIDDLE EAST

BAHRAIN
Mr. Mangat Rai Rudra
Flat No. 12, Building No. 645
Road No. 2107, Manama 321

ISRAEL
Mr. Michael Yaniv
Moshav Sde Nitzan 59
D.N. Hanegev 85470

KUWAIT
Mr. Vijay Kumar
Yousef AL Badar Street Salmna
Block 10, Flat #8, Bldg 28

U.A.E.
Mr. Mohanlal Badlani
Radha Soami Services Center
P.O. Box 37816, Dubai
☎+971-4-339-4773

BOOKS ON THIS SCIENCE

SOAMI JI MAHARAJ
   Sar Bachan Prose (The Yoga of the Sound Current)
   Sar Bachan Poetry (Selections)

BABA JAIMAL SINGH
   Spiritual Letters

MAHARAJ SAWAN SINGH
   The Dawn of Light
   Discourses on Sant Mat
   My Submission
   Philosophy of the Masters, in 5 volumes
   Spiritual Gems
   Tales of the Mystic East

MAHARAJ JAGAT SINGH
   The Science of the Soul
   Discourses on Sant Mat, Volume II

MAHARAJ CHARAN SINGH
   Die to Live
   Divine Light
   Light on Saint John
   Light on Saint Matthew
   Light on Sant Mat
   The Master Answers
   The Path
   Quest for Light
   Spiritual Discourses, in 2 volumes
   Spiritual Heritage
   Thus Saith the Master

BOOKS ABOUT THE MASTERS
   Call of the Great Master—Daryai Lal Kapur
   Heaven on Earth—Daryai Lal Kapur
   Treasure Beyond Measure—Shanti Sethi
   With a Great Master in India—Julian P. Johnson
   With the Three Masters, in 3 volumes—Rai Sahib Munshi Ram

INTRODUCTION TO SPIRITUALITY
   A Spiritual Primer—Hector Esponda Dubin
   Honest Living—M. F. Singh
   The Inner Voice—C. W. Sanders

Liberation of the Soul—J. Stanley White
Life is Fair: The Law of Cause and Effect—Brian Hines

BOOKS ON MYSTICISM
*A Treasury of Mystic Terms, Part I: The Principles of Mysticism
(6 volumes)*—John Davidson
The Holy Name: Mysticism in Judaism—Miriam Caravella
Yoga and the Bible—Joseph Leeming

BOOKS ON SANT MAT IN GENERAL
In Search of the Way—Flora E. Wood
Living Meditation: A Journey beyond Body and Mind
—Hector Esponda Dubin
Message Divine—Shanti Sethi
The Mystic Philosophy of Sant Mat—Peter Fripp
Mysticism: The Spiritual Path, in 2 volumes—Lekh Raj Puri
The Path of the Masters—Julian P. Johnson
Radha Soami Teachings—Lekh Raj Puri

MYSTICS OF THE EAST SERIES
Bulleh Shah—J. R. Puri and T.R. Shangari
Dadu: The Compassionate Mystic—K. N. Upadhyaya
Dariya Sahib: Saint of Bihar—K. N. Upadhyaya
Guru Nanak: His Mystic Teachings—J. R. Puri
Guru Ravidas: The Philosopher's Stone—K. N. Upadhyaya
Kabir: The Great Mystic—Isaac A. Ezekiel
Kabir: The Weaver of God's Name—V. K. Sethi
Mira: The Divine Lover—V. K. Sethi
Saint Namdev—J. R. Puri and V. K. Sethi
Saint Paltu: His life and teachings—Isaac A. Ezekiel
Sarmad: Martyr to Love Divine—Isaac A. Ezekiel
Sultan Bahu—J. R. Puri and K. S. Khak
Tukaram: The Ceaseless Song of Devotion—C. Rajwade
Tulsi Sahib: Saint of Hathras—J. R. Puri and V. K. Sethi

BOOKS FOR CHILDREN
The Journey of the Soul—Victoria Jones

For Internet orders, please visit: www.rssb.org

For book orders <u>within</u> India, please write to:

Radha Soami Satsang Beas
BAV Distribution Centre, 5 Guru Ravi Dass Marg
Pusa Road, New Delhi 110005